Sit 25 May
Sat 2nd June

9th June
10th June

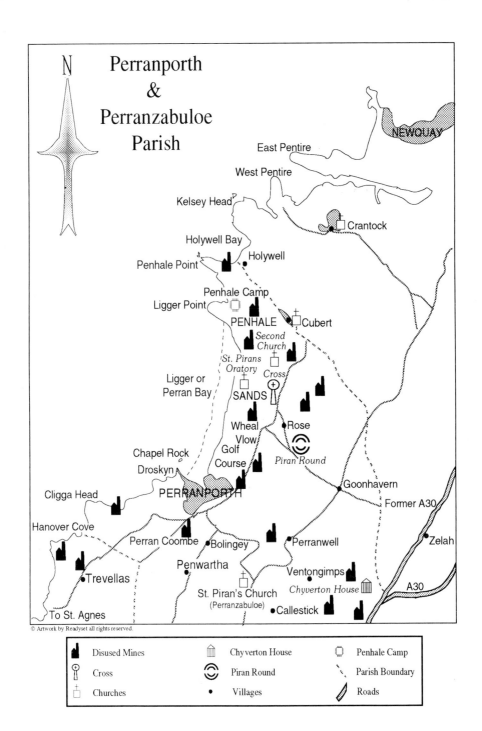

Perranporth
&
Perranzabuloe
Parish

N

NEWQUAY

East Pentire

West Pentire

Kelsey Head

Crantock

Holywell Bay

Holywell

Penhale Point

Penhale Camp

Ligger Point

PENHALE

Cubert

Second
Church

St. Pirans
Oratory

Cross

Ligger or
Perran Bay

SANDS

Wheal
Vlow

Rose

Golf

Piran Round

Chapel Rock

Course

Droskyn

Goonhavern

Cligga Head

PERRANPORTH

Former A30

Hanover Cove

Zelah

Perran Coombe

Bolingey

Perranwell

Penwartha

Ventongimps

A30

Chyverton House

Trevellas

St. Piran's Church

Callestick

To St. Agnes

(Perranzabuloe)

© Artwork by Readyset all rights reserved.

	Disused Mines	🏛	Chyverton House		Penhale Camp
	Cross	◎	Piran Round		Parish Boundary
	Churches	•	Villages		Roads

PERRANPORTH
AND PERRANZABULOE PARISH

by

Bill Trembath

Lodenek Press

First Published 1992
© Bill Trembath, 1992

ISBN 0 946143 20 X

Published by Lodenek Press, Portloe, Truro, Cornwall
Tel: (0872) 501736

In association with The Strand House, Perranporth.
Tel: 0872 573219

Typeset by Readyset, Porthglen, Hental, Perranporth, Cornwall. Tel: (0872) 572030
Printed by Booth Bookbinders Ltd, Antron Hill, Mabe, Penryn, Cornwall. Tel: (0326) 373226

CONTENTS

	Page
Foreword by Donald R. Rawe	5
Acknowledgements	7
1. PERRANPORTH - THE NAME	8
2. PERRAN BAY	9
3. THE BEACH IN THE FORMER DAYS	14
4. HOLIDAY MAKING	20
5. SAND THE INVADER	25
6. THE LOST ORATORY-CHAPEL OF ST. PIRAN	28
7. THE MODERN CROSS	37
8. PERRAN ROUND	39
9. SMUGGLING	40
10. ROCKS AND LANDSCAPES	41
11. MINES AND MINING	42
12. SOME SHIPWRECKS	51
13. PILCHARDS	61
14. SOME PARISH TALES	64
15. BOLINGEY INN	69
16. CHYVERTON HOUSE	70
17. CALLESTICK	74
18. VENTONGIMPS	78
19. MARAZANVOSE	79
20. GOONHAVERN	80
WALK No. 1: Perranporth Beach to Holywell Bay	85
WALK No. 2: Droskyn to Cligga Head, Hanover Cove and St. Agnes	93
WALK No. 3: St. Piran's Church to Penwartha Coombe	99
WALK No. 4: Perrancombe—Cligga—Droskyn	104
References	109

FOREWORD
by
Donald R. Rawe
(Bard *Scryfer Lanwednok*)

My personal associations with Perranporth and district go back nearly sixty years, to when we would travel down from Padstow on a Sunday afternoon in my father's Morris Cowley, to wander about the fabulous beach and among the rocks, and have tea at the beachside cafe. Those were haclyon days, it now seems, when the tourist trade was quiet, and there was time without pressures or problems - at least as far as we children were concerned.

In 1970 I had the chance to put on one of my plays, *Petroc of Cornwall*, at Piran Round. In the wake of the 1969 Ordinalia production there by Bristol University, we scored a considerable success. In 1971 my play *The Trials of St Piran* was performed at the same venue. There can be no greater joy for a writer and producer of plays than to see his work come alive in such a marvellous setting and atmosphere. In 1970 I was made a Bard of the Cornish Gorseth, also in Piran Round. Today I am gratified to see the Round being so devotedly cared for by the people of Rose.

In 1979 I became involved, along with Professor E.W.F. Tomlin and the Revd. Royle, in trying to save St Piran's Oratory-Chapel from burial. We failed, perhaps, to alert the general Cornish public to the danger. Ladbroke's, the owners of the site, had been most co-operative; we were on the point of launching an appeal through various Cornish organisations when the Perranzabuloe Parish Council accepted the offer and advice of the Department of the Environment and had the site covered in sand 'in order to preserve it.' This, I have always felt, is rather like locking the Mona Lisa up in a bank vault. We must hope and pray that better times will come and the money will be found to excavate the little church - so dear to our memory and significant as the earliest place of Christian worship on mainland Britain.

Meanwhile the Lowender Perran Inter-Celtic Festival had been launched, and I became a supporter of it from the first, holding stalls and selling Cornish Tartans and books over some twelve years at the Ponsmere Hotel. Also at the Ponsmere, I have often participated in the twice-yearly Conference on Cornwall, which has done much to examine specifically Cornish problems and highlight them to the public and the authorities. I have made many friends among the business community, the writers, antiquarians and artists of Perranporth. I have come to know the delightful outlying parts of the parish, so much ignored by those who have come to think of Perranporth itself and its beach as the main attraction.

Which brings me to exactly why this book is so valuable a contribution to our knowledge of Cornwall. Encapsulated here in one parish is a whole panorama of typically Cornish history. Examples of everything the Duchy has to offer exist in Perranzabuloe.

Bill Trembath, who came from Essex of an old expatriate Cornish family, has spent some fruitful years finding his own roots and delving into the nooks and crannies of the past. Mining has been his obsession, and no parish was more concerned with it than this. Today it has all been tidied away, perhaps too successfully; but it is still there under our feet as we walk the street of Perranporth, in the dunes, the hills surrounding, hinting of its presence only by the remaining refuse or 'attle' heaps, and the odd engine house chimney such as at Budnick and West Chyverton. Amongst other things this book is a worthy memorial to the vast endeavours of Cornish miners of a departed age.

Perranzabuloe and Cornwall have long needed this book. I am sure it will meet with the response it deserves.

ACKNOWLEDGEMENTS

I particularly wish to thank Trustees and Curator of the Perranzabuloe Folk Museum, Ponsmere Road, Perranporth, for their permission to reproduce a number of rare photographs from their archives. The Museum has been built up in recent years into an excellent collection of items of local and historic interest. Along the many displays are finds from two shipwrecks in the bay, and the illustrated story of the unearthing of a wartime Spitfire fighter from under the tidal sands; plus much material on mining operations in the parish. No visitor to the area should leave without seeing the Museum, which is one of the best of its kind in Cornwall. It is open Sunday to Friday from Easter to mid-September.

I must also acknowledge with gratitude the help of many people and organisations who have given freely of their material, knowledge and memories. During the preparation of this book I was privileged to talk to Mr Bobby Mitchell, who sadly died recently. He was a much loved teller of local stories and an authority on the village of Perranporth. Special thanks are due to Mr Derek Rule and Mr P. Williams of Goonhavern, the late Revd. F.P. Royle, and to the following who provided information and lent photographs from their own collections: Mr and Mrs Tom Mitchell; Mr J. Benney; Mr and Mrs John Roberts; Mr and Mrs George Kent; Mr Nigel Holman; Mrs D. Mitchell; Mr G. Prior; Mr Jack Ingrey and Mr Steve Cull; the Curator of the Royal Institution of Cornwall, Truro; and the Cornwall Archaeological Unit; and lastly, but by no means least, I wish to thank my wife, Judith, for her unfailing interest and encouragement.

BILL TREMBATH

1
PERRANPORTH - THE NAME

'Perran' is derived from St. Piran, who is reputed to have come over from Ireland: he settled here and became patron Saint of Cornish tin miners. 'Porth' is a Cornish word meaning a Landing Place. Other local examples of this are Porth Joke, Porthtowan and Mawgan Porth near Newquay. 'Perranzabuloe' is the ancient name for Perranporth and is still the name of the parish. It comes from Sabulo, which is Latin for sand; so Perranzabuloe is St Piran-in-the-Sands.

2
PERRAN BAY

Perranporth is rightly famous for its magnificent beach. It is nearly 3 miles long and consists almost entirely of pure sand. The beach itself has been voted Best Beach in Britain in a Sunday Express poll. It certainly is one of the most scenic and impressive in the whole kingdom. Most visitors will become familiar with the middle section of the beach where the cafeteria and surf club are located. It is important for one's own safety to observe strictly the flags which show where it is safe to bathe.

EASTERN BEACH
Heading further away from the town, the cliff juts towards the sea. This is Cotty's Point, also known as Flat Rocks. From here the beach continues for another mile and a half, up to the eastern cliffs in the distance. At the back of the beach nearest Cotty's Point are the High Cliffs. The clifftop footpath offers some glorious sea views, and at sea level there are echoing caverns and caves.

The view to the west includes three headlands: from left to right, Cligga Head; St. Agnes Head; and 25 miles away, Clodgy Point, with St. Ives visible on a clear day. Walkers who complete the trip to the end of the beach will have the chance to find some colourful shells and pebbles, and to enjoy some exhilarating scenery. However, always remember to allow plenty of time so as not to be cut off by the incoming tide.

WESTERN BEACH
Less well known is the area of the beach under the western cliff, known as Droskyn Cove. It is separated from the rest of the beach by the river, and by a wonderland of rock arches and stacks known as Sunny Corner. The cliffs are dotted with the evidence of mine tunnels.

Access is also available at the far end via a flight of 70 hair-raising steps cut into the rocks. This is located directly below Droskyn Castle Hotel. The visitor descends on to a rock platform, where there are fascinating rock pools containing mussels, limpets and tiny fish. Great care must be taken to leave in good time, because, as the tide turns, the sea races rapidly in to cover the whole area.

VIEWING PLATFORM
For a panoramic view of the beach and the rocky coastline, pay a visit to the view point near the Youth Hostel at Droskyn Point. It is well worth negotiating the inclined path, and several benches are provided en-route. The wave-lashed rocks below are a favourite haunt of seashore birds like oystercatchers and turnstones. For the less energetic, there is a seat beside the Youth Hostel.

THE POLDARK NOVELS

Some memorable descriptions of the beauty of Perranporth beach are in the Poldark novels, which were written by Winston Graham when he worked here in a cabin by the sea: for example,

'They walked miles together...sometimes on the sand at the sea's edge, when the waves came lumbering in, sending up mists of iridescence from the broken heads...She walked swiftly beside him and her hair blew about her face and the wind stung colour into her cheeks.'

And: 'Now and then she paused to stare out over the beach. The sea was very quiet under the hot sun. Faint airs moved across from time to time, brushing gentle shadows over it as over the down of a bird's wing. Where the water was shallow, its surface was an ever-shifting pattern of mauve and bottle-green wrinkles.'

THE EARLY DAYS OF BATHING

In the early 1800s, August Bank Holiday was the day when the older people from Truro came to paddle in the sea. Bathing was not then fashionable. Paddling was regarded as a special treat. One lady said, as she dried her feet with a pocket handkerchief: "I do come to Perranporth once a year on Bank Holiday as regular as clockwork, to wash my feet whether they need it or no." The Victorian Age ushered in the patent Bathing Machine, and a local man, Jimmy Pump, decided to introduce one at Perranporth. His donkey hauled it to the beach every day, but bathers continued to undress in the coves as before, and Jimmy's machine was hardly ever used. He gave up and used the apparatus as a store for seed potatoes. At that time, the proprietor of the Tywarnhayle Hotel was keen to increase his trade. He had previously done well out of a party of distinguished gentlemen who had arrived to witness a ship about to be blown ashore; in the event the wreck was avoided, but the visitors had spent a good deal of money with the landlord and they got him to promise to despatch a telegram next time a wreck appeared about to happen. He and his pals devised a plan. They captured Jimmy's bathing machine at the dead of night, together with the potatoes, and set it on the sand dunes in full view of the town.

Next morning they cabled the distinguished visitors with the message, "Ship signalling distress, come quickly." The expectant visitors lost no time in arriving and they demanded to see the wreck. However, at the same time, Jimmy Pump arrived and swearing vengeance, he set off with his donkey to retrieve the so-called shipwreck.

The visitors adjourned to the hotel to drink to their fill, after which they climbed aboard their coach and horses outside the front of the hotel. The proprietor rushed out waving the unpaid bill. There was no response with cash, only a cheery "Goodbye" and loud laughter. The scheming landlord was left standing in the porch, a sadder but wiser man.

INNER BEACH

In days gone by, the sea extended further inland. The Beach Car Park was part of the shoreline where boats were hauled out of the water, and the present Green next to the Car Park was the Inner Beach.

CHAPEL ROCK

The main landmark in the middle of the beach is Chapel Rock. Erosion by the sea is steadily reducing the size of the rock.

One story is that the people of St. Agnes buried their dead here before their own chapel was consecrated. The Cornish name for Chapel Rock is Angarder, The Chair, or Hermit's Station. There was a very ancient chapel here, reported to be still visible in 1733. It was probably the home of a devout monk who lived alone. This was common on islands across the Western Celtic world. The early Celtic church of 400 A.D. to the Middle Ages included many such hermits who hung on in the most lonely and weather-bound conditions.

Main beach, with Chapel Rock.   *(Photo: Steven Cull.)*

In 1922 the foundations of a building were discovered, along with some roof slates. Afterwards the centre of the rock caved in and no traces remain today.

A similar rock with the same name is at Bude in North Cornwall, which also was inhabited by a hermit. At Lelant, near Hayle, the name of the village comes from Lan-anta, or Chapel Anja, probably the name of the hermit who inhabited another rock in that estuary, lighting fires and ringing a bell to warn sailors of the dangers it held for them, as they navigated that stretch of the river.

General view, main beach, with Gull Rock in distance. (Photo: Jack Ingrey.)

RIVERS ON THE BEACH
Streams are often called rivers in Cornwall. Two rivers run on to the main beach and merge together. The larger of the two is the Ponsmere River flowing from the east, and the other is the Perrancombe River, from the west.

The Ponsmere (Great Bridge) River used to cross the middle of the beach and meet the sea on the other side of Chapel Rock. It fanned out in the shape of a wide delta. This arrangement made much of the beach unusable. The town's improvement committee acted to divert the river into its present channel so that it could be bridged. In winter, storms and high tides have been known to completely change the course of the river and leave the foot bridge with nothing but sand underneath.

GULL ROCK
Also known as Carter's Rocks, Gull Rock is the island standing offshore at the far end of the eastern cliffs. From Perranporth, it appears as a single rounded rock, but seen side-on from Holywell Bay, it emerges as a pair of steep-sided islands. A fierce current sweeps in between, making landfall by boat a difficult manoeuvre; but even so an iron ring was installed for mooring visitor's boats.

Nesting seabirds used to make a deafening noise in spring and until recently, during spring and summer, there were burrows full of puffins - known locally as 'sea parrots.' The waters around the rocks are favoured for lobsters, crayfish and crab. The only soil lies on the slopes facing inland. The modest cover of grass once encouraged a farmer to graze sheep there, but they perished in the winter gales.

MAN AND HIS MAN

Looking out to sea in a westerly direction are two upright rock outcrops. These go by various names: Man and his Man; The Cow and Calf; or Bawden Rocks. They were formed of hot granite bursting out from beneath the earth some 275 million years ago, and, being much harder than the surrounding rock, they have weathered the battering of waves far better over the aeons.

The rocks are an important breeding site for the sea birds that nest on tiny rock ledges – shags, kittiwakes, guillemots and razorbills.

3
THE BEACH IN FORMER DAYS

The oldest known photograph of Perranporth, about 1850, showing mining sites. Droskyn engine house on skyline. Note shape of Chapel Rock, as compared with today.

Perranporth, centre, in 1910. The railway in foreground, with the Tywarnhayle Hotel beyond it.

TREATS

Bank holidays were big events for the local population, when villagers would gather for a day out on the beach. Picnics on the Flat Rocks were a favourite pastime and a welcome relaxation from hard labours. Enterprising individuals arrived with wagons carrying tanks of hot water, ready for the tea drinking which was always one of the highlights of a Cornish treat.

SNAILS

Before the present Promenade Hotel was built, vegetable gardens were laid out there. The gardener was in the habit of picking out the snails as he dug. When he had a handful of snails, he would absent-mindedly toss them over the side. One day the snails landed on a freshly painted water-colour of an artist. Local people were highly amused when instead of cursing, he simply said "Oh dear."

View looking up St. George's Hill about 1890.

WRECKING

Out at sea, the busy shipping lanes into the ports of Wales and the Bristol Channel have resulted in useful items washing up on local beaches. Perranporth people have been keen beachcombers or, to use the old word, wreckers. Wrecks were a regular event in the days of sail-powered ships, and when cargo was carried on open decks, interesting finds were always coming in on the tide.

Candles were a local speciality one year. Cases containing 25 lbs of candles each were washed up and at certain tides the beach was littered with loose candles. They were

The beach below Droskyn Castle Hotel.   *(Photo: Steven Cull.)*

The descent to Droskyn beach.   *(Photo: Steven Cull.)*

foreign made and they burnt clearly and evenly. The village people stored away enough altogether to last them through three winters. The women were said to have pulled down their blinds during the daytime and burned candles because they were 'cheaper than daylight!' Probably this was to keep the houses warmer on cold winter days.

The cliffs beyond Droskyn.   *(Photo: Steven Cull.)*

Great lengths of timber often came ashore, and these were dragged off and used in the building of the first shops and work sheds. Under the huge weight of the wet wood, horses and carts could get bogged down in the sand and it would be touch and go to dig them out before the tide surged in.

In the period up to World War I, anyone taking anything from the beach had to dodge the Coastguards, one of whose jobs was to prevent smuggling. They kept look-out from a hut on top of High Cliffs.

SEAGULLS
Seagulls are often all lumped together in one's mind, but several species are to be seen here and around Perranporth.

There is always a gathering of gulls on the river in front of the Beach Car Park. These are mostly Black–headed gulls small gulls with red legs and chocolate brown heads if in breeding plumage, or with a brown mark behind the eye if not breeding. Also present are the much larger Herring Gulls with big webbed feet and a red spot on their bills. These greedy and aggressive birds are the most numerous gulls nearly everywhere. The young birds are mottled brown.

Out near the sea, the largest gulls, the Greater Black-Backed Gulls, are seen in ones and twos. Strangely enough, the Common Gull with greenish yellow legs is quite a rare visitor. Birdwatchers will be searching for rarities such as the Glaucous Gull and the Mediterranean Gull. Along the clifftops, you can look down and see Fulmars - handsome small petrels with straight grey wings and snow white heads, pastmasters at using the thermals and other air currents for gliding.

Rock pool at base of cliff, Droskyn. (Photo: Steven Cull.)

COAL SHIPS

Although there is no harbour here, ships from Wales used to arrive at Perranporth with coal to power the mines. They often encountered great difficulties in landing. In 1879, for example, there was great excitement and everybody ran to the cliffs to watch a coal vessel approach. The barque could not enter due to the state of the tide. It failed again in the evening, and it was the next day before the tide came in smoothly and left the ship sitting on the sands. Unloading could take several days, the coal being hauled by carts across the river.

TIN PROSPECTING ON THE BEACH
The cliffs everywhere are riddled with tin workings. The sand itself had also been worked for tin. Whenever the beach was churned up by north winds, black and brown tin ore residues were left behind on the edges of hollows in the sand. These deposits were raked into piles and taken by cart to dressing floors inland, where the tin could be flushed out. Despite the impurities the tinners made a living.

Beach tin was also blown against the foot of the cliffs. A gang of six tinners would dig a deep pit or 'puddle' in the hard sand and use three planks in a V-shape to funnel water into a sieve, with a treacle tin positioned underneath. The valuable tin ore, being heavy, fell towards the middle and the sand ended up at the sides. A special wide shovel was used for 'vanning', that is, whirling the shovel about in water until a beautiful brown streak of tin showed at the shovel edge. This was the signal to lift out the concentrated tin or 'crop' and then sell it to the smelting house.

4
HOLIDAYMAKING

THE FIRST TOURISTS

Tourists have been visiting Perranporth since at least 1800, when it became fashionable for Truro people to take the waters. Then, about 1850, visitors from further afield began to undertake tours. Wilkie Collins, writing his 'Rambles Beyond Railways', came here in 1851, and wrote about Piran Round and its plays (see chapter 8).

Droskyn Castle hotel shortly after its construction

The Castle hotel today   *(Photo: Jack Ingrey.)*

Lower Liskey Hill, about 1920.

The celebrated poet, Lord Tennyson, enjoyed the quiet charm of old Perranporth, staying at Hampton's Cliff Cottage for three months. He roamed over the cliffs, beach and dunes, and composed various verses praising the virtues of the area.

The first true guide book, Murray's for Devon and Cornwall (1851), included Perranporth: 'Much geological interest in the coast. Perranzabuloe has an Inn and is a small bathing place on a sandy cove.' The newly exposed oratory-chapel of St. Piran is described, but otherwise Murray considers this a desolate place. In 1880, Tregella's *Tourist Guide to Cornwall* says: 'The Tywarnhayle Arms affords homely accommodation.' The fine beach, the Oratory and Piran Round are the main attractions, all fully described. A walk back to Truro is recommended, through unfrequented lanes. Tregellas' 1890 edition states that 'a few lodging houses are being built'.

In the same year *The Thorough Guide to Devon and North Cornwall* reports that Perranporth is growing; the Perranporth Hotel (no longer existing) is highly recommended, but the village is still small and straggling. We are warned that bathing near the cliffs can be dangerous.

The arrival of the railway in Perranporth in 1903 opened the door to holidays for many more families.

BATHING CONVENTIONS
In Victorian times modesty prevailed, and bathers covered most parts of their bodies. Ladies wore bathing costumes which had bloomers to the knees. In 1876, at a meeting held at the Public Room, Perranporth, it was suggested that, looking to the increased number

21

Chapel Rock, about 1900.

of visitors at this popular watering-place, it was desirable, for the convenience of ladies especially, to lay down rules for bathing. A Resolution was passed - 'That the Western Beach be reserved exclusively for gentlemen up to 9 a.m. and for ladies exclusively from 9 a.m. to noon.'

BED AND BREAKFAST

One of the first ladies to offer bed and breakfast accommodation one day received a letter enquiring about her facilities and asking about her W.C. All she could think of for W.C.

Scene from Droskyn, about 1935.

Rough plank bridge over stream, 1950.

was the Weslyan Chapel, at the village of Bolingey. So she wrote back saying that the nearest W.C. was half a mile away and contained seating for 600 people.

Black's *Guide to Cornwall* (1919) remarked that 'the little watering place of Perranporth (Perranporth Hotel, etc.), 8 miles from Newquay, has been much in favour with Truro excursionists, and begins to come into wider notice as a haven of refuge from the "madding crowd." 'The cliff and cavern scenery is very fine, all the more as in contrast with the adjacent dunes. From Chacewater, near Truro, a railway branch goes across to Perranporth and on to Newquay.'

The age of popular motoring began in the 1920s and grew during the 30s, 40s and 50s, further encouraging the growth of the resort. There were also much improved bus services, and long distance coach services and tours. Ward Lock's *Red Guide to Cornwall*, published in more than fifteen editions over the years, carried a whole section on motoring in Cornwall, suggesting numerous trips. The following introductory information on Perranporth, dated 1952, gives us a nostalgic glimpse of the 'young resort', still then served by the branch railway (which was closed in 1962).

Banks. Barclays and Lloyds.
Open Monday to Friday during season.
Winter months, Monday and Thursdays (10-1) only.
Bathing. Excellent.
Firm hard sands extend for about 3 miles at low tide. Danger notice-boards should be heeded.
At low tide bathing is unwise and the vicinity of the cliffs should be avoided.
Some of the best surf-bathing in England.
Buses. To Truro, Redruth, Newquay, St. Agnes, etc.
Car Park adjoining sands, 1s.0d.
Cinema. The Palace, opposite Boscawen Gardens.
Distances from Perranporth by road:-

	Miles
Newquay	9
St Agnes	4
St Piran's Round	1
Cubert	4
Truro	9
Perranzabuloe	2
St Piran's Lost Church	2
Crantock	6

Early Closing Day. Wednesday.
Entertainments. Cinema; dances at the Women's Institute, etc.
Billiards at Men's Institute and Conservative Club. Reading room, etc., at
Men's Institute, adjoining beach.
Summer Repertory Theatre.
Excursions. During the season British Railways
issue cheap day return tickets to nearby places of interest.
There are also coach tours to beauty spots.
Golf Links. 18-hole course on the cliffs eastward.
Visitors' fees: 3s 6d. per round; 5s per day (including Sunday);
£1 per week; £1 10s. per fortnight; £2 10s per month. Tel. Perranporth 2161.
HOTELS.
Perranporth. Sully's. Ponsmere. Tywarnhayle Droskyn Castle. Droskyn House.
Boscawen. Bay. Headland. Penlenna (Guest House).
Places of Worship and hours of Sunday services:
St. Michael's, 8, 10, 11, 6.; Methodist Chapel, 11 and 6;
Catholic (Christ the King), Holy Mass, 9.30 Sundays, and Holy Days.
Population. Approx. 3,400.
Post Office. 9 a.m. to 6 p.m.,
Wednesdays 9 a.m. to 1 p.m., Sundays 9 to 10.30 a.m.
Putting and Bowls. Boscawen Gardens, where is a Boating Lake.
Railway Station. On Truro and Newquay line, about mile from sea.
Visitors should enquire here regarding Cheap Tickets to other beauty spots on the line
(Tel.: Perranporth 3211).
There is also a halt known as Perranporth Beach which is slightly nearer to the sea.
Road Route: from Newquay via Trenance Valley and Trevemper Bridge.
The Perranporth road bears right after 1 mile (A3075). At centre of Goonhavern turn right.
Tennis. Perranporth Lawn Tennis Club open to visitors.
Eight grass courts. Sunday play, from 2 p.m.

5.
SAND THE INVADER

WIND BLOWN SAND

For many centuries, the sand has been trying to take over at Perranporth. The ocean crushes millions of rocks and shells into tiny particles which are then thrown up by wave action to form the beach. The wind sweeps up the loose sand and blows it inland to form massive dunes. Thus a huge dune complex has developed, stretching from Perranporth, 5 miles to Holywell Bay in the north. Similar dunes occur at Hayle, near St. Ives, along the Camel estuary, and at the lost villages of Margam and Nicholaston in South Wales.

Sand dunes near the village, 1948.

In 1584 the traveller and writer John Norden reported that the parish was 'Almost drowned with sea sande, that the north weste winde wherleth and driveth to the lande, in such sorte, as the inhabitants have been once alredye forced to remove their church, and yet they are so annoyde, as they daylie loose their land.'

The Cornish geographer and historian Richard Carew in his *Survey of Cornwall*, 1602, explained how only running water could stop the sand's progress:
'This parish but too well brooketh his surname "in Sabulo", for the light sand carried up by the north wind from the sea shore, daily continueth his covering and marring the land adjoined, so that the distress of this deluge drove the inhabitants to move their church: howbeit when it meeteth with any crossing brook, the same by a secret antipathy restraineth and barreth farther encroaching that way.'

25

MARRAM GRASS

Today the sand is anchored by the growing of marram grass, the roots of which reach down through the dunes and hold them in place. Sir Walter Ralegh is said to have introduced marram grass to Perranporth. He was related to the Cott family who were Lords of the Manor in the late 1500s, and he informed them of the identical grasses in Virginia, U.S.A. where he was engaged in colonising for the British.

During World War II the beaches and dunes were laid with explosive mines in case of invasion. Planting the mines and then removing them caused new erosion by the wind. The problem has been solved by new areas of marram plantation which are fenced off whilst they become established.

THE LOST CITY

Legend tells us that beneath the dunes lies buried a great city called Langarrow, said to have been the greatest settlement in ancient Britain. The story goes that it was buried by sand in a colossal storm which lasted three days and nights, as a punishment for the excesses and evils of its inhabitants.

Evidence comes from the 16th century historian Nicholas Rocarrock. He wrote that nearby Crantock Church, 'had of olde seven churchyards belonging unto it. And several Parishes did use to come yerelie into it... bringing with them Relickes and placing them on seven stones like Aulters.'

THE DUNES TODAY

The dunes now play host to a wide range of activities. The northern half, called Penhale Sands, is an Army training area. Access is limited to the coastal footpath around the clifftops, and signs tell walkers to watch for the flags that denote when firing is in progress, in which event the path cannot be used.

The rest of the dunes are not restricted in the same way. There are car parking spaces on the road between Mount and Perranporth, and from here paths reach out towards the historic site of St. Piran's Lost Church, the nearby church ruins and the Celtic Cross. Further west are Gear Sands, occupied by a group of caravan parks. Nearest the town are Reen Sands, the home of Perranporth Golf Club. The course was laid out in 1928 by James Braid, a famous golfer and distinguished designer in the golfing world.

RARE FLOWERS

The crushed shell fragments mixed with the sand give rise to a high content of lime - 3 cwt per ton. Unusual plants grow in the lime, e.g., Hairy Rock Cress, Hoary Plantain, Greater Hawkbit, Babington's Leek, Houndstongue, Quaking Grass, Sand Catstail, Hairy Buttercup, Common Gromwell, and Dune Fesque.

CHOIR PRACTICE

At the turn of the century, a young carpenter used to practice his hymn singing as he came home from work. One dark evening, he stood on top of a sand hill and loudly sang, 'The Trumpet Shall Sound,' from Handel's 'Messiah'. A local washerwoman, on her way home, overheard this dramatic rendition, and was found crouching, calling out, 'Don't 'ee, don't 'ee, don't 'ee.' Hardly surprising, because the hymn goes on, 'In a moment, in the twinkling of an eye, at the last trump: for the trumpet shall sound, and the dead shall be raised incorruptible, and we shall be changed.'

6.
THE LOST ORATORY-CHAPEL OF ST. PIRAN

ST. PIRAN

Deep in the dunes lies St. Piran's oratory, the famous 'Lost Church.' Pilgrims have been coming here for nearly 1500 years. Its atmosphere was summed up by Canon Doble: 'At the lonely oratory amid the sand hills, we feel more than anywhere else , that we are treading in the footsteps of one of the makers of Christian Cornwall. Everywhere in Cornwall are the names of Celtic saints who founded our churches, but here we see, undisturbed by later associations of Gothic churches and modern homes, the spot where one of them lived, still to some extent as it was in his time.'

St. Piran (pronounced *Pirran*) is said to have been the greatest of the many Irish saints who came to Cornwall as missionaries in the 6th century, though Professor E.W.F. Tomlin in his book 'In Search of St Piran' holds open the possibility that he was a native Cornish saint. Certainly Cornwall came to rival Ireland as the Land of the Saints, and there were said to be more saints in Cornwall than in Heaven. Lyrical names like St. Endellion, St. Wenn, St. Mellion and St. Enoder, appear among the hundreds of holy hermits and teachers who lived and worked here during the fifth, sixth and seventh centuries A.D.

THE ORATORY TODAY

Visitors to St. Piran's Oratory will see it has been covered over under a mound to protect it from decay. Placed on top is a granite slab inscribed with the words:

THIS STONE IS DEDICATED TO THE GLORY OF GOD AND IN MEMORY OF SAINT PIRAN, IRISH MISSIONARY AND PATRON SAINT OF TINNERS, WHO CAME TO CORNWALL IN THE 6TH CENTURY.

BENEATH THIS STONE IS BURIED THE ORATORY WHICH BEARS HIS NAME, ERECTED ON THE SITE HALLOWED BY HIS PRAYERS.

October 1980.

An oratory is a small room for one's own private devotion. Strictly speaking the building was bigger and catered for a small congregation; it should be called a Chapel, but the name Oratory has stuck. Professor Tomlin refers to it as the Oratory-Chapel of St Piran. The low-lying hollow at the foot of the mound was prone to flood and to damage the oratory. But we must remember that a source of fresh water was important to St. Piran and his followers. Their well was regarded as a sacred place: thousands of brass pins with hollow heads have been unearthed here. They date from the 14th century onwards. It was the practice for young girls especially to throw a pin, usually a bent one, into a well or spring, and to say a wish at the same time. Another tradition was for girls to fix two inch-long pieces of straw together with a pin, so making a cross, and drop it into the well. The number of bubbles coming to the surface told girls how many years would pass before they would be married.

The Oratory Chapel with railings, before the concrete shell was built.

Every Cornish saint had a holy well. St. Gulval's well was used by people hoping for news of absent friends. It ran clear if the friends were well, or muddy if they were dead. St. Ludgvan's well could cure dumbness and poor eyesight and keep at bay the hangman. Its miraculous powers came to an end when the Devil spat in the water. St. Nest's well had three fish in it, the Saint would take one each day for his meal, but there were always three next time he came.

THE SECOND CHURCH
Nearby to the east, across a sand-choked channel, are the ruined foundations and low walls of the Parish Church built in 1100. This building itself was abandoned in 1805 because of sand-drifts, and included the remains of a second ancient oratory. (See Walk No 3.)

THE CELTIC CROSS
Standing near the site of the church is a Celtic Cross, one of the best and tallest preserved in Cornwall. It has the typical wheel-like head, but strangely one of the four holes has not been punched right through. The exact age of the cross is unknown, but it is at least 1000 years old. It is referred to in a charter of 960 A.D. as 'Cristes-mace'.

The cross was probably a boundary marker indicating the outer edge of the sanctuary, an area where criminals on the run could take shelter, safe from arrest. It also no doubt served as a preaching station before the second church was built. Crosses were usually 1000 paces away from the shrine of a saint. This one is 800 paces away, having been moved at some time in its long history.

The Celtic cross, one of the most beautiful and best preserved in Cornwall, standing as a landmark near the Old Parish Church. It is referred to as 'Cristesmace' in a charter of 960 in King Edgar's reign.

LEGENDS

Many legends surround the life of St. Piran. We can estimate he was born in Ireland in about 540 A.D., though one dating puts his birth at about 480-A.D.

He was reported to have crossed to Cornwall on a millstone, to which the King of Munster had bound him, cresting the waves like a modern-day surfer. In real life, he probably sailed in a simple boat called a coracle, and the millstone was the little portable altar stone which he would insert into the communion table. Such altars have been found up and down Cornwall; one is now preserved in the Lady chapel wall of St Merryn church, near Padstow.

St. Piran is reputed to have performed the miracle of feeding ten Irish kings and three armies for ten days using only three cows. He bought back to life dogs killed whilst hunting and revived dead warriors on the battlefield. Even so, the king condemned him to be thrown from the cliffs. A crowd rolled a huge millstone to the top of a hill and Piran was chained to it and rolled over the edge. The sky was dark with clouds, but when Piran was airborne, the sun shone and the sea became as smooth as a mirror. This miracle converted hundreds to Christianity, and St. Piran floated on to Cornwall, where he was said to have lived for 206 years and visited Rome to become a Bishop.

Another story credits the saint with the discovery of tin smelting. One evening, whilst he was cooking his supper over an extra large fire inside a cave, a large black rock he was using as a hearthstone split open, and a shining white liquid ran in lines across the floor. This cooled to form the tin metal. (In actuality tin had been smelted since the early Bronze Age, 2,000 years previously.)

The flag of St. Piran has become the Cornish National Flag. It is a white cross on a black background and depicts white hot tin metal issuing from the black rock. More heroically, it stands for the light Christ shining in a dark world.

THE LONELY SAINT

Why did St. Piran choose such a lonely place? He was not alone in doing so. Ireland was a centre of early Christianity, well before much of Britain was converted. The main Irish missionaries came across and spread their message, they often chose very isolated settings.

Best known is St. Columba on the Isle of Iona in the Scottish Hebrides, and there were similar foundations at Lindisfarne off the Northumberland coast and on the Isle of Man. Even tiny rocky islands were chosen and their occupants lived on them as hermits. So St. Piran was part of a wider movement of missionaries living close to nature. They were following in the footsteps of the 4th century Egyptian hermits who retreated to the deserts, and whose eccentric life had led to anchorites establishing themselves all round the coast of North Africa, Spain, Brittany, Ireland and Scotland.

HISTORY OF THE ORATORY-CHAPEL

The present building under the sand was constructed about 800 - 900 A.D., and seems to have replaced St Piran's original oratory, possibly even including some of the stonework. It was first engulfed by sand and abandoned about 1050 - 1100. Another chapel was built on the site of the second church, which the Normans enlarged into the Parish church about 1100 -1150.

From time to time, the first oratory-chapel was blown clear of sand. It may then have been used, as was the church of St. Enodoc near Padstow, which the priest and worshippers entered through the roof, when it was partially buried in the 19th century.

The second Church of St. Piran in the Sands. (Artist's impression by Alice C. Bizley.)

A VICTORIAN EXCAVATION

The oratory-chapel was excavated in 1835 and 1843. The findings were described in a letter from William Michell to the local newspaper:

'This church is probably one of the most ancient ever laid open. It is as complete as when first erected, except for its roof and doors. At the eastern end is a neat altar of stone. Above the altar is a recess, in which probably stood a crucifix, and on the north side of the altar is a small doorway, through which the priest must have entered...The congregation were accommodated with stone seats attached to the walls. In the centre of the south wall, is an extremely neat Saxon arch-way, highly ornamented. The key stone of the arch is rudely sculptured with a tiger's head. The floor was composed of sand and lime, under which bodies were buried; the skeletons of two having been discovered. It is remarkable that no vestige of a window can be found...It must be presumed that the services must have been performed by the light of tapers. Around this interesting building lie thousands of human bones exposed to desecration; the winds having removed the sand in which they were deposited.'

We are lucky to have this account of the lost church and its cemetery. The sand had preserved them from alteration for a thousand years.

THE CEMETERY

The bones of the wind-blown graveyard made the sand appear white. In 1820 it was reported that, 'thousands of teeth and other human bones, even whole skeletons, lie exposed in regular order.' In 1835 the Cornish Quaker diarist Caroline Fox visited the scene of the oratory-chapel and noted 'the curious church of Perranzabuloe, where we found a great quantity of human bones and skulls.' Later in 1910, the skeletons of a woman with a child in her arms was unearthed near the oratory doorway. The burials have led historians to believe that St. Piran was interred in the oratory or that the chapel was built on top of his tomb. This is because it was ancient practice for people to have themselves buried as close as possible to the bones of a holy man.

RELICS AND PILGRIMS

The Victorians found some remarkable relics at the oratory-chapel. The holes for the roof rafters were still intact, and some of the plaster clung to the walls. The large doorstep at the south doorway was well worn with the tramp of feet, as were the steps above and below. More remarkable still, three headless skeletons lay under the altar and the skulls were hidden away nearby. One of the skeletons was exceptionally large. The tradition was that St. Piran was a very big man, and so it was said that the saint's body had been discovered.

This may or may not have been true. Later in 1910 it was reported that a skull with skin attached had been found 9 feet below the surface and surrounded by five flat stones. This may have been one of the relics of the Saint, or of another holy man, which in medieval times were transported from place to place for the veneration of people in different towns and villages. After the Reformation this practice was outlawed and the skull may then have been buried in a hurry. From the 9th to 15th century, the remains of saints were paraded on tour and this raised a good deal of money from alms. Nicholas Rocarrock (1600) wrote: 'I who was born...not far from St. Piran, remember his relics were wont to be carried up and down in the country, and to have seen them so carried in the time of Queen Mary.'

The relics consisted of head and leg bones. They were kept in a niche above the altar and the sacred vessels, the paten, chalice and flagon, in a cupboard below the altar. In 1269, the first vicar of Perranzabuloe was appointed, and his living was partly financed by the display of relics. In 1281, St. Piran's head was kept in a special reliquary 'bound with Iron and locked'. Then in 1433, the will of Sir John Arundel of Trerice near Newquay provided money for a new casket to house the head. Throughout the middle ages, St. Piran's shrine was esteemed more than any other in Cornwall. On his Feast Day (March 5th) pilgrims came from as far as Brittany to declare their devotion. Indeed, the people of other towns complained that St. Piran's relics were drawing away visitors and income. Bodmin for example, earned considerable alms from the bones of St. Petroc.

The oratory was a central point of the Pilgrim's Way, stretching from Ireland to Spain. Padstow was the arrival point for pilgrims from Ireland, Wales and the North. Mousehole and Penryn on the south coast were departure points for Santiago de Compostella in Spain. Pilgrimages to Perran Sands have continued into the 20th century.

STONE FIGUREHEADS

Three stone mouldings decorated the south doorway. One of these is thought to have represented St. Piran, and another his mother Wingella. The third looked like a tiger or leopard or a wild cat, and it may relate to the medieval idea that St. Piran's first followers were animals, like those of St. Francis of Assisi.

After a tourist had damaged two of the figureheads by poking them with his stick, replicas were made and placed in the Royal Institution of Cornwall, Truro.

These three heads were positioned over the south doorway. Replicas were later made of them.

THE WORLD OF ST. PIRAN

The oratory or church as excavated by the Victorians is dated 9th century, and could not have been built by St. Piran because he lived some 300 years earlier. Nevertheless the site is almost certainly the same one used by the saint, and the shape of the building may also be the same. St. Piran chose to settle in a sheltered valley near a spring and stream. Green grass no doubt grew all around before the sand encroached.

His first buildings would have been of wattle and daub, and then later, a wooden structure. We cannot expect these to have survived, apart possibly from post-holes in the ground, but the stone-built church that lies buried today may well contain parts built by the saint's disciples.

ORIGINAL BUILDINGS

The oratory was surrounded by other scattered buildings, all forming St. Piran's monastery and settlement. Professor Tomlin writes:

'In its heyday, the complex may have contained half-a-dozen monks' cells, a refectory, a storehouse or barn, a mill for grinding corn, a guest-house, a scriptorium where manuscripts were copied and even a small school.'

The buildings were all small and cramped, amounting to little more than huts. A cemetery was also begun. A hundred yards to the south east was a hut called St. Piran's cell. In 1835, a wooden door-case survived and at its threshold, mussel and limpet shells were found, along with earthen pottery. An old drawing shows a cottage near the old parish church. It may have been the monastic guest-house and later, an inn. As such, male and female visitors may have lodged there, and so it was placed away from the monks' place of worship.

LANPIRAN

The monastery settlement was called Lanpiran. In Cornish *Lan* means an enclosed Christian monastic community. Lanpiran became a manor in its own right, with an abbot as the head of the community. There are references to Lanpiran in the Saxon charter of 960, and in the Domesday Book of 1083, when its area amounted to 360 acres.

A survey of 1281 shows Lanpiran had become prosperous, helped no doubt by income from the display of relics. Amongst the possessions listed were St. Piran's staff, 'ornamented with gold, silver and precious stones'; some teeth of St. Brendan; and a tooth belonging to St. Martin of Tours, in a silver pyx.

A photo of the 1920s, showing concrete shell built in 1910.

35

DEVELOPMENTS SINCE 1895

The Ecclesiastical Commissioners sold the whole site in 1895, and the new owner handed it to a Trust in 1905. A fund of £500 was raised for preservation, and further excavations took place. The oratory–chapel was found to be based on a large plinth. In 1910, it was housed in a massive concrete block structure resembling an aircraft hanger. The public gained access from openings at the front. Throughout the 1920s conducted tours were organised and occasional services were held.

Then serious flooding occurred and the concrete cover deteriorated; some vandalism took place during and after World War II. The Trust could not live up to its duties, and the property was eventually sold to Ladbrokes, who owned the neighbouring holiday camp. In 1976 a committee met to decide how best to preserve the fragile remains, but it was not thought practicable to raise sufficient funds to drain and rehouse it; Perranzabuloe Parish Council were persuaded that only complete burial would suffice, and so it was covered in with an artificial hill by the Department of Environment in 1980.

The whole monastery area has now been donated to the parish council. One day, we may hope it will be re-excavated and revealed once more to the public. Such is the chequered history of one of the earliest surviving Christian monuments in Britain.

7.
THE MODERN CROSS

Visitors to the Oratory will be guided to the spot by the large concrete cross which sits atop a nearby sand-hill.

The cross was erected in 1969 at the instigation of the then Vicar of Perranzabuloe, the Revd. F.P. Royle. He had been inspired by a trip to Switzerland where hilltop crosses are often put up, in order to mark the memory of the dear departed.

The purpose of the Perranporth cross was to act as a waymarker for the guidance of visitors to the oratory. People had often become lost in the dunes, especially in misty weather. Previously, about 1963, the Revd. Royle had overseen the erection of a wooden cross, constructed from timber donated by Lord Falmouth. Unfortunately, after some three years, the cross was sawn down in an act of vandalism.

The modern cross of concrete, erected by Truro Rover Scouts. *(Photo: Steven Cull.)*

A local building contractor offered to make a replacement cross which could not be destroyed: it was to be of concrete. The builder manufactured this gigantic cross in his own garden. Being all of one piece, it was to prove difficult to move to its intended site.

The Royal Navy from RNAS Culdrose were asked if they could possibly lift it into position by helicopter. However, they assessed its weight at 40 tons and thus beyond their capabilities. After languishing in its place of birth for nearly three years, the cross was finally moved into position by the Army in an epic manoeuvre.
Revd. Royle was also Chaplain to the Penhale Army Camp. He met a Colonel of a battalion of the Royal Engineers whose motto was "Anything is possible." The challenge of moving the cross was taken up, and a special tank-retrieving vehicle was brought in for the task. It travelled by road from north-east England on a bank holiday. Questions were asked in the House of Commons as to why such a slow-moving vehicle should be allowed to hold up the traffic all across the country!

Upon arrival at the builder's home, various boundary walls were demolished to allow access for the machine and its precious load, but the mission finally succeeded. The cross was erected by the voluntary effort of the Truro Rover Scouts. The result is a monument built to stand the test of time.

As we have seen, during the 1970s efforts were made to ensure the survival of the oratory itself. However, to his deep regret, it was buried some years after Revd. Royle retired from the incumbency of the parish.

8.
PERRAN ROUND

One of the curious local antiquities is Perran or Piran Round at Rose, just off the road between Perranporth and Goonhavern, where a circular earth embankment surrounds a flat inner area. It dates from late Iron Age and Roman periods, and is probably 2000 years old.

Rounds were the typical Cornish settlements of that period. They sheltered oval–shaped stone houses within a simple bank and ditch, mainly for defence against either invaders like the raiding Irish Kerns, or animals such as wolves and bears. The evidence suggests the homesteads were rebuilt several times throughout the life of the Round.

During the Middle Ages, the Round was adapted for use as a *plain-an-gwarry* : place of the play, or open air theatre. Audiences came from all round to enjoy the Cornish miracle plays, at Corpus Christi. Rows of seats were cut into the surrounding banks. In modern

Perran Round, showing the Devil's Spoon depression. (Photo: Steven Cull.)

times, these ancient dramas were revived again (1969 - 1973) and both the *Ordinalia* Cycle, and *Gwryans an Bys* (The Creation of the World) were performed here.

In the middle of the Round is a pit eight feet wide, known as the Devil's Spoon. Local legend says that if one runs round the pit twelve times and then puts one's ear to the ground, one can hear the sound of the Devil below frying souls. It was probably built to be covered with brushwood so that, during the Creation scenes, God the Father could create Adam and Eve and the animals by apparently raising them from the ground.

9.
SMUGGLING

Organised smuggling was a feature of life in Perranporth into the late 18th and early 19th centuries. Even the most respectable citizens were involved in its daring adventures. Smuggling was encouraged by high duties on wines, spirits, tobacco, salt, sugar, tea, and silk. The penalty for being caught was often a long sentence of penal service in Australia. The Revenue men patrolled the coast, on foot and horse-back on land and in sailing cutters at sea. At Perranporth, the caverns under the cliffs were used to land the contraband out of sight of the Customs men. In 1780, the vicar and other leading men of the village formed a secret smuggling syndicate. They acquired a fast ship to trade direct with Cherbourg in France; in fact *Cherbourg* was the name of the ship.

When the *Cherbourg* arrived under cover of night, she would be signalled to a rendezvous with smaller craft so that the goods could be transferred. Small boats were steered to one of two very dangerous landing sites: either Cligga Porth, a tiny steep-sided cove near Cligga Head, or Vugah-En-Plunder (west of Droskyn Point) where there were two large caverns large enough to take several rowing boats at a time. It was 80 feet from the cave roof to the surface above, so a shaft was sunk, up which goods were handled by rope and pulley. Mules would be standing by, ready to carry the bounty in panniers along a cart track.

The *Cherbourg's* speed was famed, and she often outsailed the Revenue patrol boats. Unfavourable tides and winds sometimes stopped her from unloading, and the kegs of spirits had to be lashed to a raft or tied to a grapnel so that they could be picked up later. At these times, it was worthwhile to search the beach to see what was washed up.

All went well until one day when the smugglers got wind that the Customs Officers had arrived in the village just at the time when a load was being brought ashore. One boat had already discharged its cargo and the contraband was hidden under one of the ricks of dried gorse, used for winter fuel. The officers passed to and fro by the rick but did not think of looking into it.

Nevertheless, the game was up; and the *Cherbourg* was pursued by a Revenue cutter and fired on repeatedly. She scraped into Cherbourg, two miles ahead of her pursuers, only just out of gun range. Very likely, the Customs had been tipped off in the first place. Suspicion fell upon a new member of the smuggling syndicate. Nothing was proved, but later when this man built some new cottages, many people thought his money came from a government bribe, and the cottages were nicknamed 'Cherbourg Row.'

10.
ROCKS AND LANDSCAPES

The majority of rocks in the area are of mudstone, shale, slate and sandstone laid down about 350 million years, when Cornwall was covered by sea. These rocks have been twisted, shattered and folded by later earth movements, and heated and chemically altered by contact with hot rocks injected into them.

About 300 million years ago, a huge reservoir of molten granite welled up beneath Devon and Cornwall. It broke through to form Dartmoor, Bodmin Moor, and the other smaller granite areas including a small exposure at Cligga Head, west of Perranporth town. This intense activity gave rise to swarms of mineral veins containing tin and other ores throughout the Perranporth area. White veins of milky quartz show up in the cliff faces as seen from the beach.

The present landscape owes much to invasion by the sea 12 million years ago. The water smoothed the land into a level plain, but a later uplift of the earth has produced the present plateau at 400 feet above sea level. In turn, steep-sided valleys have been carved out by rivers far larger than those of today. The retreat of the sea and the uplifting of land can be traced to the Ice Age, when a high proportion of the world's oceans were frozen into glaciers and gigantic sheets of ice over a mile high.

11.
MINES AND MINING

MINING IN PERRANPORTH

For 150 years before Perranporth became a holiday resort, mining dominated the landscape and brought employment. Hundreds of miles of galleries and tunnels lie beneath the main street, under the dunes, the cliff and much of the town.

Tin, copper, iron, lead, zinc and silver were all brought out. The saying goes that far more lies undiscovered than was ever mined. The visitor of those days would have seen a scattering of cottages and farm houses, with the working engine houses clanking away, the great chimney stacks sending up their plumes of smoke, surrounded by massive piles of mining waste. The site of the present car park behind the main street, and of the tennis court and boating lake, were mining areas with engine houses, dressing floors, and heaps of mining waste called 'churk.' An elevated aqueduct spanned the hillside. A local author, Captain Roberts, wrote, 'It would be difficult to convey to the modern visitor an idea of the landscape in 1870. All the wastage caused by the mining operation still remained. True, all mining machinery and equipment had been removed, as had all saleable material, leaving only the gaunt but stripped engine houses with their high chimney stacks and the roofless mine buildings, to render the scene one of desolation: to say nothing of the unsightly and immense accumulation of waste rock in hillock form.'

Wheal Alfred mine at Perranporth.

42

Working conditions in the mining age were appalling, often involving a four-mile walk to and from the mine; 8-hour shifts; a descent down 2000 feet long ladders; dripping water, wet clothes, foul air, dust and powder smoke. Miners aged 40 were already old men who wheezed and struggled for breath. Children aged eight to twelve worked at the surface, and older boys worked Sundays. Women worked as bal maidens, sorting out the ore.

'Wheal' is the Cornish word for a mine-working; many relics still remain in the district. Two-thirds of the world's copper production came from Cornwall in the years 1800-1830, earning the Duchy the name of The Copper Kingdom. Decline set in during the years up to 1880, mainly due to cheaper and more accessible sources of copper abroad, but the industry around Perranporth collapsed sooner than was necessary (see under Individual Mines: Wheal Leisure and Perran Great St. George). Cornish miners emigrated in their thousands to the four corners of the world, and became the mainstay of hard–rock mining in U.S.A., Canada, Mexico, Australia, and South Africa.

Perranporth, about 1905, with Wheal Leisure mine and fish cellars, centre.

PRESENT DAY REMAINS

The engine houses have all been dismantled for building materials, but the landscape around St. Agnes, the next parish west, gives a good idea of what Perranzabuloe looked like in the heyday of mining. A stack of chimney remains at Budnick, by the entrance to the Sports Club to the north of the village, and an overgrown spoil heap can also be detected in the fields beyond. The cliffs at beach level are riddled with miners' excavations. Drainage pipes of cast iron still discharge on the beach. At Sunny Corner across the river from Chapel Rock, the coastline is peppered with tunnels, and the cliffs are divided into stacks by the effect of collapsed galleries.

These workings under Droskyn Point are very old. The land is honeycombed with tunnels to the depth of 90 feet below sea level. Two large recesses were cut to house the water wheels, measuring 50 feet in diameter, which pumped the shafts dry. The coastal path to St. Agnes is flanked by scores of old mine shafts, many of them on the very cliff-edge, showing how men worked in the most dangerous places imaginable.

CLIGGA

About a mile west of Perranporth is the Cligga area, next to Trevellas Airfield where the Gliding Club is situated. The remnants of the explosives factory built in 1891 are to be seen here (see Walk No.2). The 19th century Cligga mines were connected inland to the valley of Perrancombe by a narrow gorge which is now a public footpath. Water was pumped through to power the mining machines in the valley below. The channel was named 'Susan Tregay's Droke', after its owner. Susan's son, William, became a wealthy man in Australia and rose to be Mayor of Melbourne in 1850. (See also Walk No. 2.)

As the development of the Cligga Mine progressed a larger headgear became necessary. The picture shows the erection of the new headgear, and the buildings of the treatment plant in progress.

INDIVIDUAL MINES

Many local mines go back to a time before records were kept. Their known history is nonetheless fascinating. The sand-hills north-east of Perranporth are the setting for a series of ancient mines, mostly medium-size producers of tin or lead, unlike the big copper mines under the village itself. The dunes also house the Great Perran iron mines. Starting at the village end of the sand-hills, near to Ponsmere Bridge, the mine of North Wheal Leisure incorporated the even older mines of St. Catherine, Good Fortune, St. Matthew, Rostilban, and Wheal Vor. In 1830, a drive into St. Catherine Lode provided large amounts of tin but work was halted by a slide.

Later the lode was picked up again by one Captain Gripe. His shaft was to be sunk into soft, running sand; he used an iron casing and a pneumatic apparatus pumped by four men. The inventor was Dr. Lawrence Holkar Potts, who was the physician at the Cornwall Lunatic Asylum. Sand and water were sucked out as the iron casing slid down, 'Amidst the wonder and gratification of the bystanders which a pause in activity allowed, the friends of science in the neighbourhood had the pleasure of witnessing the results.'

To the seaward side was Wheal Ramoth, extending to the edge of the beach near the surf club. It included the very ancient mines of Wheal Mehal, Wheal Bude and Wheal Perran. One of its three lodes is believed to continue across the bay and into Droskyn Mine. Working ceased about 1830 due to bad drainage, but ruined buildings stood until recent times.

In the middle of the dunes at Gear Sands were yet more ancient mines, Wheal Creeg and Wheal Vlow, and a mining village since drowned by sand. The mines were drained by half-mile long adits, issuing onto the beach. Records begin in the 1700s, and tin was being sold during 1803-18. Then in 1835, these mines and others inland were grouped into the Perran Consolidated Company, one of whose directors founded the Johnson Matthey Bank. By 1838, Perran Consols employed 100 men. Wheal Vlow was worked for tin until 1874; efforts to re-open it in 1927 failed. The mine is now dwarfed by Perran Sands Holiday Village; during its working life it stood isolated in the windswept sands. It was this image of Wheal Vlow that led Winston Graham to use it as the model for Ross Poldark's own mine. Just to confuse matters, he named it after a very different local mine - Wheal Leisure.

Further along the sand-hills, a quarter of a mile on from the Lost Church, lay Wheal Mary, where five shafts tapped the seams of lead. Little survives because the buildings were taken down in 1860 to be re-used at nearby iron mines.

The story of mining in the dunes now transfers to the Great Perran Iron Lode, which cuts through the sand-hills from one side to the other, and to the Iron Boom of 1850-1890. At the sea cliffs is Gravel Hill Mine, which also included nearby Big Iron Pit. A hill cliff railway drew out 8,000 tons of ore in the peak years of 1874-1882. One mile south-east is Halwyn Iron Quarry with an unfinished tramway. Another five hundred yards along the lode is Mount Mine or Perran Iron Mine. Production included 38,000 tons during 1859-76. It was studied by the Government's Home Ores Department during World War Two, and a limited amount of iron was extracted for the war effort. For many years, Perranporth's water supply came from this mine, much to the consternation of the engineers who serviced the pumps whilst a seemingly bottomless chasm lay beneath.

The iron lode progresses inland and out of the dune country. Three of the most productive mines, Treamble, Great Retallack and Duchy Peru, now the setting for a secluded caravan site, enjoyed three phases. During the first, from 1859-1892, shafts were sunk and 16,000 tons raised. Then in 1937, modern plant was moved in by Lloyd's Perran Iron Co. and the land stripped for opencast working. Unfortunately, the lode, instead of being the expected 40 feet wide, was exposed as a mere 14 feet. Nonetheless, 4,000 tons were yielded. Underground mining was resumed and, under Government control, 15,000 tons produced to help win the war.

Treamble's third claim to fame is its fuller's earth, which was refined at the on-site mill and transported on the purpose-built rail branch line (The Mineral Railway to Newquay) from 1874 to 1949. Up to 500 tons a year was sold: a profitable by-product of the iron lode. This was discovered as a soft material, talcy to the touch and sometimes white, cream, yellow, pink, or red. One deposit ran for half a mile and was up to 80 feet wide. It is thought to have been formed by the action of natural sulphuric acid decomposing the older rocks. Up to 500 tons a year of fuller's earth was sold for refining vegetable oils and as a filler for cement, paint, rubber and bitumen products. Next door was Great Retallack Mine - a big iron producer and also a major source of zinc. Duchy Peru, south-west of Rejerrah village, was the largest and deepest of all the iron mines. The lode here is 60 feet wide and over 300 feet deep. Records include 32,000 tons of ore during 1858-86.

The Iron Lode is a remarkable geological feature; its mines have produced over 200,000 tons of iron ore. As long ago as 1710, John Woodward had written, 'The vein has been worked formerly and is vastly large.'

Returning towards Perranporth past the golf course, the town's one remaining mine chimney-stack stands at the foot of the hill near the sports club. The mines of Wheal Budnick and East Leisure drained to the spot, and the running water powered a stamps and buddles for processing rock ore. Well into the present century, freelance miners brought ore here by horse and cart. Budnick Mine stretched to Rose village and its mixed yield included lead, copper, and tin.

The prosperity of Perranporth as a mining village came largely from the two great copper mines underlying what is now the built-up area: Wheal Leisure; and Perran Great St. George, an amalgam of five smaller mines. Their heyday was the middle years of the last century. Miles of galleries lie beneath the village.

The two mines were loosely divided by the Perrancombe river. Wheal Leisure was to the east, its engine-house and centre of activity just to the south of the main street. Its workings descended to 700 feet below ground level, and consistently large volumes of copper were extracted, with over 60,000 tons of ore from 1829 to 1840. Large reserves lie untapped at greater depth and out under the sea. An imposing Count House stood at the junction of the main street and Ponsmere Road. The owner, Captain John Oates, rose from the ranks to become a wealthy man with a summer residence at Cot House - later extended to become

Ponsmere Hotel - as well as a winter home at Rose-in-Vale, Mithian, now a country restaurant. Upon his death in 1855, he bequeathed £600 to the parish, the dividend to be shared: 'For ever, unto some of the poorest, most industrious and most deserving settled inhabitants.' An average of £12 is still distributed each year around Christmas.

The village's other major copper mines were amalgamated into the vast sett of Perran Great St. George, which stretched from the centre of the village and the cliffs, south-westwards to Cligga Head, a distance of two miles. Three separate lodes ran parallel to the coast. The original mines were Wheal Droskyn, Wheal Perran, Perran United, Perran St. George and Great St. George (also called Good Fortune). Droskyn in particular has a long history dating back beyond the 1500s. Indeed some long-forgotten workings are now covered by the sea. The Cornish name of Droskyn, after which the Point, Cove and mine are named, comes from the word *dreskeyn* meaning 'crosswise' - or 'across the back' - a reference to the way veins lie at an angle.

In one part or another of the Perran St. George sett, mining continued for an unbroken spell of 200 years. The copper veins proved highly productive, and yields have included two

Mine adits under Droskyn.

47

unique slabs of native copper which were sent for display in the British Museum.

Much of the evidence of mining activity has been obscured as the village has expanded, but at Droskyn Point the cliffs are peppered with tunnellings; around the cliff-path the shafts and tailings are evident; and at St. George's Burrows near Cligga, there is a landscape dominated by weathered stacks of mine waste. Formerly, for example, the valley floor now occupied by the boat lake and tennis courts were part of the working area of the Perran United mine.

Perranporth's two central mines were not good neighbours. After years of dispute, in 1870, Wheal Leisure sued St. George's for encroaching into its lodes. The courts found against St. George's and fined them £20,000. In retaliation, St. George's ceased to operate and closed down its pumps, thus flooding the Wheal Leisure workings and effectively ruining the local copper industry.

Some 2,000 jobs were lost and a period of deprivation and emigration followed. At this time, the village was everywhere covered in heaps of mine waste, and the vicar, Reverd. Parkhouse, devised a scheme to use up the waste and employ the destitute miners. In this way, between 1877-79, 200 men were put to work building a new highway across the marshes from Perranporth to Bolingey. The men who queued for work each morning received 1s.0d. a day as against the normal daily wage of 2s.6d. Their monument is known as New Road.

A mile to the south-west of Perranporth, Cligga Head Mine is situated close to the headland cliffs, and is driven into the granite outcrop. In addition to tin, the scarce mineral of wolfram has been found here and mined ready to be made into tungsten. The granite is penetrated by hundreds of thin veinlets of ore.

The high cliffs were once worked by primitive shafts and tunnels, but the mine has a more recent history. In 1938, ore was being raised and then processed by water power in Perrancombe. Then in 1939, the Rhodesian Mines Trust Ltd. took over and sank shafts to sea-level. Zones of economically viable ore were located, but not sufficient to start opencast working. Instead, conventional deep mining was used, and the mine came into its own during the war, producing 300 tons of wolfram concentrates. This venture closed in 1945.

Since the war, the mine has been prospected a number of times by a succession of different companies. In 1962, Geevor Tin Mines Ltd. erected a headgear and ancillary buildings. The main shaft, Contact Shaft, was sunk a further 200 feet and a drive made seawards. This spell of prospecting lasted until 1965. Again, in 1972, International Tin Services spent several years sampling the mine. As recently as 1985, Concord Mines proposed to re-open

Railway gangers wth engine near Perranporth 1920.

the mine, but the plans were dropped when the tin price suddenly collapsed, making working no longer viable.

THE MINERAL RAILWAY LINE

A railway branch line was built to Treamble Mine in 1874 to carry iron ore from the Great Perran Lode to Newquay harbour, from whence it was shipped for smelting to South Wales, where it was prized for its purity. The line was further extended to Gravel Hill Mine near the beach, but this section survived only till 1888.

This very scenic railway line served to bring out fullers earth for valuable wartime needs. Commercial traffic ceased in 1949, and the track was pulled up in 1956. The stone built pillars survive where the railway bridges formerly crossed the roads in the Rejerrah area, and are fine examples of the mason's art of stone work.

PERRANPORTH AS A MINING TOWN

Perranporth became an important centre for copper mining, which gave work to thousands of men, women and children. Wages were paid every month on a fixed day; the town came alive on pay day.

The centre of the community was the Tywarnhayle Hotel and the nearby bridge. Tywarnhayle was too much of a mouthful so the hotel was referred to as the Tavern. People greeted each other with, "Going up (or down) Tavern?"

Tavern came to mean not just the inn. It was the place for business transactions, sport and open-air amusements, and refreshments on pay day. At that time (early to mid-19th

The village about 1920; note railway in foreground and Penhale mine on clifftop.

century) there were virtually no permanent shops; instead the forecourt of the Tavern was spread with all sorts of merchandise, stalls, booths, cheapjacks, fortunetellers, pedlars and so on. These monthly gatherings included, as Captain Roberts wrote, 'The usual drunks, fights and oft-times domestic infelicity.'

12.
SOME SHIPWRECKS

Like most of the Cornish coast, Perranporth has seen its share of dramatic wrecks and heroic rescues. At least five major wrecks occurred from 1870 - 1895, during the age of the sail power. Ships with their sails damaged became trapped by the winds in the area of sea between two headlands and could not rejoin the open seas. Their only option would be to head for a soft landing on Perranporth beach.

The ALMA. One Sunday morning, 2nd March 1873, during a terrific gale, the *Alma* appeared with all her sails blown away. She was from Ireland on route to Portsmouth with a cargo of oats, beef, and butter. The ship grounded near Chapel Rock, the 4-man crew took to a boat, and were thrown into the surf.

They were rescued by the coastguards throwing life-lines and two men on horseback who threw their whiplashes for the sailors to grab. One local man rode his pony deep into the surf to drag out the cabin boy. The oats were carted to a temporary store in a fish cellar. At night, for every two loads to the cellar, one load would find its way to the carrier's own barn.

The wrecked ship laid on the beach for months until broken up for firewood. A good many oats were left over to be dispersed by the sea. For years afterwards, self-sown oats grew round the fringe of the beach like a green border.

Remains of the wreck of the La Seine near Chapel Rock.

51

The HANNAH LOUISE was a coal ship from Chepstow on passage to Padstow; she was blown off course on 1st August 1879, and beached on the east of Chapel Rock. Wisely the crew stayed aboard and were safely rescued. The ship was stranded for some months and then emptied of cargo; she was refloated but was still leaking. A tug was used to tow her into Padstow for repairs; the crew reboarded, along with a deck hand from Perranporth, and resumed the voyage. However, just off Trevose Head, at the dead of night she took on water and sank with the loss of all of her crew and the Perran man.

LA SEINE was a large French vessel carrying nitrate from Chile. On 27 December 1900, manned by a crew of 22, she got into difficulty and the newly established Perran and St. Agnes rocket brigade sprang into action. After many attempts a rocket-propelled line was secured aboard, and the crew were dramatically hauled across on to the cliff top at Droskyn Point.

Soon, this once beautiful ship lay on her beam ends, dismasted, with steel shell gutted by the waves. Later, she was sold to a Newquay sea captain for a mere £42. The wreck yielded a quantity of cups and plates which women carried away in their aprons. This coarse, heavy china was in use at Perranzabuloe for many years afterwards. Some of the remains of the La Seine may be seen near Chapel Rock, on occasions, at low tide.

The VOORSPOED: a Dutch schooner carrying sugar-refining machinery and a crew of 9. On 7th March 1901, the ship beached east of Chapel Rock and the rocket brigade secured a line. The crew did not make a move and Dr. Postlewaite, the first medical officer in Perranporth, was sent out on the line. Amid speculation that the crew were intoxicated, the doctor helped them into the carrying buoy. At first, the captain refused to leave his ship, but he was persuaded when the doctor pointed out to him the nearby wreck of *La Seine*. Once the vessel was stranded by the ebbing tide she was the subject of looting by navvies working on the G.W.R. line being built from Chacewater, but also by local men and women. The ship herself was refloated and sailed to Falmouth to be refitted, but with disastrous results, because on her first voyage to Newfoundland, she went down, never to be heard of again.

The DAUNTLESS (10 February, 1871) was perhaps the most fascinating of all. She was bound from West Africa to Bristol with a cargo of palm oil and nuts, and a crew of 14 men and an African cabin boy. When the ship struck near Chapel Rock the crew jumped into the boats and, though crippled with fever, most of them rowed ashore, steering with a broom handle and bailing with their caps. The cook and another sailor were drowned. The cabin boy stayed behind, and was found shaking with fear and suffering from exposure. He spoke only a native African tongue. A religious society took charge of him and he was sent to Bristol where he was educated, trained as a missionary and later appointed to West Africa. Before leaving to begin work, he visited Perranporth to see where he had been miraculously rescued.

WRECK GOODS FOR SALE
PERRANPORTH

For sale by PUBLIC AUCTION AT PERRANPORTH in the parish of Perranzabuloe by Mr. J. Tregoning. ON TUESDAY 28th Day of MARCH 1799, by ten o' clock in the forenoon, the following wreck goods part of the cargo of the Brig MARY, lately wrecked at Perranporth.

3 Cables of 11 to 12 inches in circumference (one being entirely new)

60 Casks Irish Butter (from one to three cwt. each)

3 Ships yards 1 Windlass 1 Topmast 2 Anchors

2 Masts 1 3–pounder Gun 1 Bowsprit 2 Anchor Stocks

1 Ship's boat, (about 24 feet long.) A large quantity of ropes and cables. **FOR VIEWING APPLY TO MR. JOHN OATES AT PERRANPORTH.**

Dated TRURO 6th MARCH. 1799

A typical auction poster of the times, resulting from a wreck.

SCHOONER MYSTERY

In the days of sail, almost anything could turn up. Captain Roberts relates how, early one morning, a sailing vessel was discovered jammed between rocks at Cligga Head with full sail rigged up. The sea had not been rough over night, and everything on board was undisturbed. There should have been a crew of four or so but there were no signs of life. The cabin table was set for dinner. A mystery on the lines of the *Marie Celeste* unfolded. It was weeks later when the word came through that the crew had previously been rescued in the far-off Isles of Scilly, and had abandoned the ship, assuming it would sink; instead it had drifted for 50 miles to Perranporth.

Green lane at Perranwell. (Photo: Steven Cull.)

The stream below Bolingey, on its way to Perranporth. (Photo: Steven Cull.)

Unique thatched cottage at Bolingey.   *(Photo: Jack Ingrey.)*

A Cornish barn with cob (earth) buttress near Pencrennow, Bolingey.   *(Photo: Steven Cull.)*

*St. Piran's church, Lambourne: the 9th century
cross by the south door.*   *(Photo: Jack Ingrey.)*

Former school at Penwartha, built in 1878.   *(Photo: Jack Ingrey.)*

Traditional Cornish cottages at Perranwell.   *(Photo: Jack Ingrey.)*

Wind-shaped trees, Reen lane.   *(Photo: Steven Cull.)*

Converted chapel (1843) and School room (1853), Perranwell.   *(Photo: Jack Ingrey.)*

Perranporth Bowling Club.   *(Photo: Jack Ingrey.)*

13.
PILCHARDS

PILCHARDS BY THE MILLION

Up to 1880, the miners of Perranporth doubled as pilchard fishermen. Millions of fish visited Cornish waters from August to November; one shoal in 1869 was 30 miles long. As many as 8 million fish might be caught in a single seine net. When word went out that a shoal had been sighted, the miners would down tools and take to the sea in one of the village's 18 boats; the rest of the population would assemble to watch the spectacle, but ready to help bring the fish ashore.

Perranporth from Sandhills, 1893.

THE HUER

The key man was the 'huer' or look-out. He was stationed on top of a cliff, and his job was to direct the boats to the shoals with flags or branches of gorse, and giving directions through a speaking trumpet. Where the water changed colour, a shoal would be present and the huer would blow a trumpet and shout "A heva! A heva!"

Heva is Cornish for 'swarming.' It gave rise to Heavy Cake, a delicious, substantial and quick cake which was eaten on pilchard days. Ingredients:- 6 ozs plain flour, 1 ozs sugar, 3 ozs currants, 3 ozs lard, teaspoon salt, peel if required.

Mix flour, salt and fat roughly together. Add other ingredients, mix with water to a stiff dough. Roll to half inch thick. Criss cross with knife to represent fish netting. Bake at 370F, (1900), gas mark 5, for 25-30 minutes.

COMPANIES

The sea at Perranporth was split into sectors based on landmarks ashore, and four companies of fishermen took turns in each zone. They had colourful names: the Union, Miners, Farmers, and the Love (previously The Cobblers).

Any trespassing into anothers company's waters was a serious crime and could lead to a dispute in the courts. It was luck of the draw which companies happened to have the fish in their area.

THE CATCH

The aim was for the huer to direct the boats into position so that their huge 1200 feet long seine net could enclose the shoal. Hundreds of excited helpers would be on the beach waiting for the tide to recede, and then:

'The net and fish were left high and dry, a high glittering wall of fish up to 4 feet thick, possibly an acre in area, and if at night time, the mass of silvery glitter, was truly a sight for the gods.' (Captain Roberts.)

It was a race against time to remove the catch before the tide returned. Everyone rallied round to shovel up the fish onto carts and wagons, using scooped wooden shovels.

FISH CELLARS

The pilchards were carried to various curing cellars in the village; there they would be stacked high between layers of salt for six weeks. The smell was overpowering as the oil seeped away. Then the pilchards were washed, salted and packed in barrels and exported mainly to Italy, but not before the villagers had made sure of their own supply for the winter. After 1880, the pilchards almost disappeared; it was a sad day, spelling the end of a great local tradition and a valuable source of income.

LAST BIG CATCH

There had been no great catches of fish for many years until 1893, when a shoal of herring was netted. Some of the helpers arriving at the beach were disappointed because they rather fancied pilchards for tea. The next day the fish were sold in Redruth. The Town Crier was up early to announce this rare treat from Perranporth.

A NOTABLE RESCUE

Courage and skill were needed to negotiate the boats in and out of the huge waves and rough surf. The master-seiners deserved their respected position, and one of them, Captain Rippon, embodied the spirit of adventure.

A farmer's boy had been sent down to the beach with a cart to fetch sand to improve the soil. He was new to the beach and unfamiliar with the coming and going of the tide. He fell asleep in a cave, and when he awoke he was trapped by incoming sea.

His cries for help were heard aboard Captain Rippon's boat. As they manoeuvred closer, the Captain called for a volunteer to plunge into the boiling surf. No response was forthcoming, so he dived overboard and swam through the heaving waves. He disappeared from sight every now and then but eventually he retrieved the boy, and was rightly hailed as a hero.

14.
SOME PARISH TALES

THE PARISH BEER-TASTER
Before the days of large breweries, every inn or 'kiddly-wink' (which was a beer-house often in an ordinary dwelling) made its own ale, and there was often great competition for the strongest brew.

At Parish Council meetings it was the custom to elect a Parish Beer-Taster. His job was to visit every hostelry and taste the ale. The lucky appointee needed an ability to judge, and 'ample capacity to retain the imbibing.'

One famous taster was only a small man, but nevertheless good at his job. As closing time approached, he would tear off his coat before the assembled company and waving his arms, announce that with his wealth, he could paper the room with five pound notes.

ROYAL CHOUGHS
The Chough is a shy member of the crow family of birds, with a scarlet-red beak and legs. For centuries it frequented the cliffs, and became a national emblem for the Cornish. The spirt of King Arthur was believed to inhabit a Cornish Chough.

In the 1970s the chough became extinct in Cornwall, although there are now plans to reintroduce birds reared in captivity. Wild birds remain in Wales, the Isle of Man, Islay in Scotland and parts of Ireland and Brittany. Perranporth used to be a stronghold of the Cornish Chough.

Two or three pairs nested in the cliffs near Droskyn Point. In 1863 a local character, Thomas Mitchell, known as Uncle Ben, made the dangerous descent and picked up two young birds, carrying them up in a handkerchief gripped in his teeth. He sent them to the Duke of Cornwall, later to become King Edward VII. Uncle Ben received a note of thanks and five pounds. For many years the choughs were on show at London Zoo, with the inscription, 'Presented by His Royal Highness to this Institution.'

PREACHING
The chapel was always well attended on Sunday. One day the elderly preacher took the text, 'There will be no night there.' He rambled on at very great length, repeating himself frequently, and oblivious of the time going by.

The congregation had listened to, 'There will be...,' so often, their patience was sorely tried. To make matters worse, it was a dismal foggy afternoon in winter. Out of the gloom, a faint voice was heard saying, 'If you don't dry up soon, it will be night here.'

Rose Wesleyan Chapel, built in 1865.   *(Photo: Steven Cull.)*

The Sabbath was strictly observed; even Sunday visits to the beach were frowned on. One fiery preacher was addressing his Sunday School class in a building in view of the shore. He happened to look up and catch sight of a group of fishermen standing at their boats. He broke off and cried, "Damn those men! Seven men down by the boats, Lord, damn them, Lord...they'll be damned!"

Methodist chapel, Bolingey.   *(Photo: Jack Ingrey.)*

GREAT ST. GEORGE MINE
At midnight on a Saturday in 1824, the boiler of the mine's south engine burst with a tremendous explosion that carried away the roof and threw down the walls. Parts of the boiler weighing over a ton were hurled a quarter of a mile. The engine man, who was on duty at the time, was crushed under a wall. He had last been seen at 10 o'clock at night, when he made his way from a nearby public house to the mine. As the local paper had it, 'It is believed he was not sober.'

SAND FOR THE FARMS
For centuries, farmers have exercised the right to cart away sand from the dunes to spread on the land for its beneficial lime content. In 1832, the Dean and of Exeter Cathedral claimed the sandhills as their property and demanded threepence a cart load of sand. They erected a fence and gate to prevent access to the dunes. The farmers were furious.

Two hundred strong men, assembled with seventy carts drawn up, and after their spokesmen had stepped forward, the obstruction was torn down and the church officials backed down.

SAMPHIRE PICKING
Rock samphire is a salty, fleshy plant that grows on the cliffs; it used to be gathered for picking as a food and flavouring.

One June day in 1813, a poor man and his wife left their 4 children at home in St. Agnes and went to pick samphire from the cliffs at Perranporth. Whilst engaged in this dangerous activity, he stood on a projecting part of the cliff; with one hand, he held part of the rock above him and with the other, he pulled the samphire which he handed to his wife who stood a few yards below him. Unfortunately the part on which he stood gave way and he fell upon the woman, both of whom were hurled down a tremendous precipice and fell to their death within 3 yards of each other. This tragedy occurred because the couple were desperate to avoid having to accept poor relief. Centuries before, Shakespeare had known all about the dangers; he wrote in King Lear:
'...Half-way down hangs one That gathers samphire, dreadful trade.'

MUSSEL PICKING
It was a custom going back to medieval times that on Good Friday Perran people would gather mussels from the rocks on the seashore. In 1838, Samuel Phillips, a sawyer at Wheal Budnick Mine, ventured too near the water as the tide was rising; a large wave appeared and swept him to his death. No fisherman or beachcomber is ever totally safe, however calm the sea appears.

STOLEN DINNERS
At the Cornwall Assizes of April, 1845, Nathaniel Lanyon was charged with assaulting Richard James and stealing from him four pasties. James, a lad, stated that he lived in Perranporth and on 11th of December 1844 about one o'clock, he was on the high road going from his labour, with four men's dinners: three in a handkerchief and one inside his coat. Two were pasties and two currant-hobbin.

The judge and lawyers were greatly puzzled to know what was meant by currant-hobbin, but the boy could not explain and seemed surprised that the learned gentlemen were not as familiar as himself with this dainty. At length, a juror explained that a currant-hobbin was a heavy paste with currants.

On his road, said the witness, he met the prisoner, who asked where he was going, whose boy he was, and what he had in his hand. The witness told him he had four dinners. The man said he was starving and would have them. The witness replied that he would be killed when he got home. The man took all the dinners and walked away, the witness went home and told his father. He afterwards gave the police a description of the man, who was apprehended a month later.

Ingredients for currant-hobbin are: 1lb plain flour, 4oz lard, 4oz currants, pinch of salt. Make up as for pastry, roll out thinly and sprinkle currants over the top. Roll up carefully like a swiss roll, and pinch ends. Bake on a greased baking sheet for 25 minutes, at 370F (190c).

PASTIES
A Perranporth woman, Mary Ann Trelease, was much sought after as a daily help. She was renowned for passing on the latest village news. If her employers asked for further details, she would say. "Well, I don't know, but I'll find out for 'ee by the next time I come."

She was not familiar with the alphabet but her pasties were in great demand. When she put several in the oven in one go, each pasty made with different ingredients, she was often asked how she remembered who the pasties were for, she replied, "Why, I mark each one with the first letter of the person's name - T for Robert and F for Phillip and so on, to be sure."

EERIE NOISES ON THE DUNES
The lonely dunes can be terrifying at night. One dark and windy night, a fisherman was crossing the sandhills with a catch of gurnards.

The Gurnard is an unusual fish; its French name is 'grogner', meaning grunter. It uses the walls of its swim bladder to make sounds varying from grunting to snoring or crooning.

It can also stay alive for a long time out of water.

The fisherman was half-way through the dunes when suddenly he heard an unearthly groan. He stood still and began to get frightened; when two or three more desperate groans followed in succession, his hair stood on end; he dropped the line of fish and ran off at high speed, reaching his home exhausted.

The next morning, he felt obliged to return to the dunes, in case he had heard the cries of someone in distress. When he rediscovered the fish, it came to him that in his days at sea, the groaning gurnards had been the most plentiful fish, and he realised that the awful sounds had been produced by nothing more sinister than a dozen fish.

THE TEMPERANCE HOTEL PROJECT

In 1870 an eccentric retired engineer built a large home near the beach. He was fond of strong alcohol, but he formed the view that two inns were enough for Perranporth. He noted the trade being done at a Temperance Hotel in Truro and determined to start one in his own village. He ordered a huge painted sign from a company in Truro.

When it was ready, he set off with horse and cart. The sign was so big it had to go cross ways across the cart. On the way back, John stopped for a quick drink at the City Inn on the hill leading out of Truro. He left the cart outside with the sign taking up most of the highway.

Whilst he was inside, the newly formed Volunteer Corps came marching up the hill, and were blocked by the obstruction. The officer in charge entered the Inn, to find John was speechless with drink. The police took him in charge, and he was returned to the town along with the horse and cart.

Some hours later, another Perranporth man was passing the Town Hall and was surprised to see John peering through the grill, beckoning to him and evidently greatly distressed. He went into the station and eventually secured John's release, so that he could start for home again.

The sign was never erected; it stood for years propped up in a nearby barn. The Temperance Hotel did not come into being.

15.
BOLINGEY INN

The Inn dates from the 17th century and is a pleasant survival from the days when Bolingey was a more important centre of population than its neigbour Perranporth. In the heyday of mining, the village supported both the Bolingey Inn and The Bounders Arms, which was a 'kiddlywink' or beer-house, situated at the entrance to Bounders Lane and now know as Elm Cottage. (*Bounder*, Cornish - Cow lane).

The Inn played a key role in local affairs. One of the main events of the calendar was the annual Perran Feast held on the last weekend of October to commemorate St. PIrran, though strangely enough his Feast Day is on March 5th, the day of his death.

Celebrations began at the pub where stalls were set up in the front yard. The assembled throng then split into two groups, one proceeding on to Bolingey chapel and the other making their way on to the Bounder's Arms. This happy occasion began to wane about the turn of the century.

At the time of the first World War, and thereafter, the inn was the venue for the Pig Club. Most local people kept a pig, fed on household scraps and whatever meal they could afford, and attendance at the pig club was vital because, for a monthly payment (amounting to ten shillings in 1939) owners could make sure of extra rations for the pigs. No club - no feed! Quite apart, that is, from the chance to enjoy the evening with a yarn and a drink or two.

Bolingey Inn. *(Photo: Jack Ingrey.)*

16.
CHYVERTON HOUSE

The large country home of Chyverton House stands amongst an estate of mature woodland in the corner of Perranzabuloe parish nearest to Zelah. Chyverton is said to mean variously 'the house upon the hill' or 'the house on the grassland'; or it might derive from *chy*, house, and fenten or venten, spring.

The present house was built in 1781 for the occupation of Mr. John Thomas, an eminent county magistrate. It was described at the time as a 'commodious and tasteful mansion' and, in the words of the Cornish historian Polsue, Mr. Thomas surrounded his new home with 'excellent gardens and flourishing shrubberies and plantations.'

Previously, the estate, with a more modest home at its centre, was originally in the ownership of the illustrious Arundell family of Trerice House near Newquay. One of their members was Sir John Arundell, a Royalist who in the Civil War defended Pendennis Castle at Falmouth at the grand age of 70; only to finish on the losing side and have his property seized for a number of years, until payment of an enormous £10,000 discharge fee.

The Arundell family's association with Chyverton came to an end in 1703 during the time of Sir Richard Arundell. The barton was sold by Lord Longueville and other trustees. The new owner was John Rosogan whose ancestors had previously held a lease on the property. In 1724, Rosogan re-sold the estate. It was bought by John Andrew of Trevallance; then

Chyverton House.   *(Photo: Steven Cull.)*

70

began a long family association of nearly 200 years. Indeed, Mr Andrew was the great-grandfather of John Thomas, and the progenitor of the Thomas - Peter dynasty which was to hold the estate into the present century.

John Thomas (1740-1825), who was responsible for the present mansion, attained the post of Vice-Warden of the Stannaries, a key position in the world of mining and the administration of the industry, retiring from that office in 1817.

Coinciding with John Thomas' period of tenure at Chyverton was the building in 1804-1805 of the new Parish Church for Perranzabuloe. The land for the Church was donated by Francis Gregor, M.P., and it was one of the duties of John Thomas, acting in the capacity of high lord of the fee, to grant consent. The costs of providing the new church were met by voluntary contributions; the list of subscribers is set out on a tablet on the north wall of the Church. Mr Thomas was a principal subscriber with a gift of a hundred guineas out of a total subscription of £786.

His connection with the Church is recognized in the naming of the south transept, the 'Chyverton aisle'. In it is a marble memorial to his wife, who died in 1768 when Thomas was only 28. John Thomas was succeeded by his daughter, an only child. She married Francis William Peter of Harlyn, and so began the Thomas-Peter family line.

F.W. Peter enjoyed a varied career, becoming M.P. for Bodmin from 1832 to 1834, and being subsequently appointed Consul to the States of Pennsylvania and New Jersey, 1840-53. He died in Philadelphia in 1853. His eldest son, John Thomas Henry Peter, was to renew the residential connection. Having begun life in Harlyn, St. Merryn, he moved to Chyverton, and pursued a distinguished career as a justice of the peace. In 1866, he became High Sheriff of Cornwall. By the time of his death in 1873, Kelly's Directory was describing Chyverton as 'that handsome modern seat.'

During the early 1900s, Captain G.F. Thomas-Peter inherited the family seat. He was a well known figure in the Truro of his day. After his mother died, the house was sold out of the family.

The new owner was Mr. A. Treve Holman of the famous family, Holman Bros. of Camborne. The prominent engineering firm is still operating as part of Compair-Holman Ltd. Continuing the traditional relationship of Chyverton with the Parish Church, Mr. & Mrs. Treve Holman generously donated the oak choir stalls in 1960.

The present owners are Mr. & Mrs. Nigel Holman; they have advanced the care of the gardens and the magnificent collection of trees and shrubs planted in the present century and before, featuring many fine Magnolias, Camellias, Acers, and exotic introductions.

Chyverton gardens.   *(Photo: Steven Cull.)*

Chyverton shares with other great Cornish houses a tradition of exotic gardens: mild conditions, deep acid soils, and thick shelter–belts of trees, combine to allow tender plants from China, America, New Zealand and all over the temperate world to prosper in a way that is unique in Great Britain.

A small stream was dammed in 1830 to form a broad pool bordered by gunnera and lysichitum. Viewed from the house, the pool is backed by a lovely Rhododendron called 'Cornish Red', planted in 1870. In his book on Cornish gardens, Patrick Synge picked out Rhododendron Schippenbachii as a personal favourite: 'an unusually fine form, in a large planting of this beautiful deciduous species with flowers floating on the bare branches like large butterflies.'

Amongst many outstanding magnolias is one named 'Chyverton'. Now some 50 feet tall, it has won an Award of Merit. Another, Magnolia Campbellii Alba, was planted in 1953 from a seed and took the relatively short period of 13 years to produce flowers. Some flowers measure as much as 17 inches across.

Mr. Holman delights in growing species new to Britain. New introductions have come with the opening up of Yunnan province in China; others are from Nepal, Korea and Taiwan. For example, there was a joint Sino - British Expedition to Yunnan in 1980, producing many interesting plants which have been brought to Chyverton to see how they fare. Many of these are too new to appear in any reference book. Writing in January 1985, Mr. Holman commented, 'By far the most attractive plant in the garden is Daphne Bholua from Nepal. It revels in the Cornish climate; in flower for two or three months, it scents the air for yards around'.

Thus in one passage, we can see the fascination of gardening in Cornwall in a woodland setting. The Cornish soil, temperature and humidity mirror the conditions found in China on the other side of the world. Evolution has favoured the Far East with some wonderful exotic flowering trees and shrubs, and their introduction to Cornwall brings great rewards.

The gardens (only) at Chyverton are open to parties by prior arrangement during March to May inclusive each year.

17
CALLESTICK.

The south-east of Perranzabuloe parish stretches all the way to the main A30 trunk road, and is made up of unspoilt woodlands, delightful minor lanes, and undulating farming country. Here in the triangle formed by the A30 and the A3075 Newquay to Redruth road, are the hamlets of Little Callestick, Ventongimps, and Marazanvose; and the country seat of Chyverton House.

The main village is Callestick (pronounced Call-*es*-tick), a tightly clustered settlement situated in the upper reach of the Venton valley, and a mile or so due south of the parish church.

Farm life prevails in Callestick, and the village is remote enough from the main centres of population to present a quiet, unaffected aspect. It has not always been so tranquil. In the last century, the village's fortunes were closely tied to the nearby mines which were important producers of Lead together with silver: most notably West Chyverton Mine, the second biggest lead mine in Cornwall, and Chyverton Moor Mine, known also as Great Callestick Moor Mine.

Callestick was home to a considerable mining population. In 1826, a Methodist Chapel was built, the first Wesleyan chapel in the whole parish, giving some indication of Callestick's size and importance in those days. The chapel was erected on the minor road leading north-west from the village, but the remains of a much earlier chapel have been unearthed at the centre of Callestick.

Callestick   *(Photo: Steven Cull.)*

Callestick *(Photo: Steven Cull.)*

For nearly 150 years, the Callestick Methodist Chapel flourished as a place of worship and served its fellow villages within the Circuit as the place of burial. Neither Perranporth nor Bolingey Chapels possessed burial grounds of their own; and hence the role played by Callestick, the long journey being a feature because of the comparative remoteness of Callestick Chapel.

In 1972, the Chapel faced a dwindling membership of only thirteen, and the prospect of a large outlay to make safe a faulty ceiling. It was decided to close it, and the building was demolished. Later, in 1985, the Methodist Schoolroom was sold at auction, with permission for conversion to a dwelling.

Although the Chapel is no more and the site is used for storage by a local builder, the burial ground to the rear is a fine survival and retains its role, still serving the wide parish. Callestick also administered to the secular needs of its mining community. Provisions were to be had at the village shop (no longer extant), and refreshment and recreation were to be found at The Albert Inn. This long-gone hostelry enjoyed a lively history throughout the mining heyday of the 1800s.

In 1872, the Royal Cornwall Gazette advertised the tenancy as follows:
To let, that well-frequented public house - The Albert Inn at Callestick, near Truro', etc. The new tenant found himself at odds with the magistrates' bench: first in 1886, being fined for allowing drinking after licensing hours; and then two years later, a similar punishment for allowing drunkenness'.
Towards the end of the century, the decline of mines emptied the area of its workers and

much of its prosperity. As a result of this exodus, the Albert called last orders for the last time in 1893.

Approaching Callestick today via one of the tiny lanes between high hedges amidst green fields, it is easy to overlook the industrial way of life that prevailed here one hundred years ago.

A network of footpaths connected Callestick to the illustrious mines that stood on all sides. These paths and tracks are mostly still there to be walked today. In a south-west direction towards Callestick Vean a footpath leads to the sites of Great Callestick Mine and Perran Wheal Virgin, which exploited a local vein of lead. To the east and north-east of Callestick, in the country lying between the village and Chyverton House were Chiverton Moor Mine and West Chyverton Mine; partial remains of both can still be seen. Chyverton Moor Mine is reached via a lane and footpath striking due east from the village. This was a long standing mine, once called Great Callestick Moor Mine. Between the years from 1847 to 1873 it produced 2000 tons of lead and 24,000 ounces of silver.

A part of the engine house survives amongst the undergrowth. This was the biggest wall in the structure, and supported a 70 inch beam engine dating from 1863. By 1870, the mine had reached a depth of 500 feet and 150 people were employed. Today overgrown spoil-heaps lie all about this well-worked site.

The neighbouring mine to the north-east was of such dimensions and wealth as to overshadow the others in the area. The West Chyverton Lead Mine employed a thousand people at its peak in 1870, in the twenty-odd years from 1859 to 1886 it yielded 45,000 tons of high-grade lead and an astonishing million and a quarter ounces of silver. Its importance as a source of lead was exceeded only by East Wheal Rose at St. Newlyn East.

The mountains of waste material testify to a long period of mining activity. The lower reaches of the tailings or waste dumps were re-sorted in the period 1917 to 1922, yielding useful tonnages of zinc which the earlier miners had not bothered to extract.

The mine is incongruously sited on the doorsteps of the Chyverton House estate; the view from the nearest road is not an elegant one, due to the infilling of the site and its use as a commercial waste tip.

Atop the hill, however, is the impressive engine house: three storeys high and a tribute to the stonemason's art. A very fine pumping engine was installed in this building in 1869. It was of such reputation that when the mine ceased, the engine was transferred to another great Cornish mine, United Mines at Gwennap.

West Chyverton mine

An unusual feature of the engine house, which marks it out from nearly all others, is the positioning of the chimney stack midway along the side wall, rather than at the corner of the house. To the east of the engine house are the derelict remains of what were the various processes for extracting lead ore from the mined rock. Firstly the tailings dam where the waste materials were allowed to settle out of the flux, and beyond, the dressing floors and the stamps used to crush the ore into fine particles.

The geology of West Chyverton at its junction with Chyverton Moor Mine has excited interest because it is one of the few examples in Cornwall where a change in rock type directly influences the distribution of metal ores.

The hot mineral-bearing magma was injected into the pre-existing 'country rock'. Normally in Cornish mines, the tin ore or other metallic ore is not confined to one particular type of country rock but rather evenly spread throughout. But here at Chyverton, as the geologist H.G. Dines records, 'The influence of the country rock upon the lode content is shown... Ore shoots are confined to bands of soft shales...and pinch out when the strata change to hard siliceous rock.'
The effect on the mining prospects is most marked. West Chyverton Mine is located in soft shaly sediment, and so is neighbouring Chyverton Moor Mine; but in between the intervening wedge of country is composed of hard sandstone and is devoid of any ore-bearing seams.

18.
VENTONGIMPS.

To the north of Callestick lies the valley and tiny hamlet of Ventongimps, an ancient place name. The derivation is from Fenton Gymps (*Fenton*, spring; *compes*, level). A local family derived their name from it: John de Fentongemps (1346).

One may park one's car near Ventongimps Mill. Opposite Bridge Cottage, the stream can be crossed by means of the 300 year old stone bridge. The way ahead leads up a slight rise to a lane on the right where we find Edwin's Thatch, dating from the 17th century: one of the oldest cottages in the parish.

The pathway beyond gives on to a road leading south; from here there are panoramic views of Callestick Moors including the gaunt house and stack of West Chiverton Mine. Close at hand in the field to the left are the ancient spoil heaps of Wentworth Consols Mine. Here is one of the few sites in the parish where Dorset Heath grows. Despite its name, it is a Cornish speciality; a many-branched low shrub with hairy stems, which flowers from June to September.

Wentworth Consuls is an old mine, presumably a producer of lead. No records survive but the main shaft has been located 550 yards S.E. of Ventongimps Mill. Today, the dumps are small, mainly overgrown, and composed of soft grey shale and pieces of vein quartz; no ore minerals are apparent.

Between Ventongimps and Callestick, the valley floor forms an important area of wetland. Unlike so many similar areas which have been drained and brought under cultivation in recent years, this is an area where wildlife and mature plants can flourish.
A reserve has been established here by the Cornwall Trust for Nature Conservation, consisting of twenty acres of woods, bog, and wild heath. The Dorset Heath is encouraged here, and the rare Marsh Fritillary butterfly has been re-introduced. In 1970, aircraft preservationists excavated the remains of a crashed bomber from the last war, and the resultant pond has created another refuge for wildlife.

19.
MARAZANVOSE.

Just south of Chyverton House, on the extreme edge of Perranzabuloe parish, lies the hamlet of Marazanvose.

Now mercifully bypassed by the busy A30 trunk road, it has an ancient history. The name is said to derive from the Cornish, *Marghas* - a market; and *An Vos* - by the wall. In this way it was a staging post on the pilgrim's way from St. Piran's Oratory to St. Michael's Mount and Mousehole, which were points of departure for Brittany and Spain. The pilgrims would have stocked up on their provisions at Marazanvose. The local route from the oratory can be traced through Goonhavern and thence by what are now lanes and paths through Carnkief and Wheal Frances in the valley southwards.

20.
GOONHAVERN.

The village of Goonhavern grew up amongst the moorlands and mines on rising ground between the coast and the high central spine of Cornwall.

The name Goonhavern has an interesting derivation. The prefix *Goon* is widespread in Cornish place names, as in Goonhilly Downs on the Lizard peninsula and more locally, Goonown and Goonbell near St. Agnes. It means moor or downs. The meaning of *Havern* is less certain. It may allude simply to a haven amidst the inhospitable moors; or it may be a corruption of a local family surname, 'Keverne'.

The earliest cottages were simple homesteads of cob and straw, possibly erected by pioneer families on the open moor. Renovations to a cottage near the village centre are said to have revealed a beam with the date 1357 carved thereon, and walls of pristine cob containing straw like spun gold.

Isolated dwellings would have been present, but an organised settlement resembling a hamlet or village did not appear until the age of industrialised mining some two hundred years ago.

The terraced cottages at the rear of the Central Stores date from mining days; one of them housed a kiddlywink or beer-house for the resort of miners at nearby Wheal Albert, a lead and zinc mine. At the heart of the village was Churchtown Farm, the farmhouse now forming one of the buildings that make up the Kernewek Pottery premises. The farm was

Goonhavern school today.　　　　　　　　　*(Photo: Steven Cull.)*

Goonhavern school juniors, 1922.

the home of Joe Nicholls, who is recalled with considerable affection; also his old carthorse called Prince.

A hundred and fifty years ago, there were about twenty dwellings in Goonhavern. To the south-east lay Polgoda Downs, an untamed wet area overlooking Wheal Frances down in the valley, (Polgoda, Cornish *Pol*, pool, and '*Gothow*' meaning geese.) Wild geese no longer visit here but it takes only a little imagination to spy a skein stooping out of a winter sky.

Goonhavern school infants, 1922.

The heart of the community was strengthened with the coming of the Board School in 1876, and the Wesleyan Chapel. Prior to the introduction of compulsory education, there were local forerunners in the shape of the little private schools where pupils paid usually a penny per week. One of them had been run by the august Mr. Tresidder, who went on to become the first Headmaster of Goonhavern School, holding the post for forty years (1876-1916). Of the same mould as the illustrious Mr. Ashworth at Penwartha School, 'Master' Tresidder ruled with a firm hand; replete with gaiters, he was a commanding sight.

Two sisters, the Misses Madge and Gertrude Pollard, both taught at Goonhavern. The housing estate called Pollard's Close commemorates them. The five Greet brothers; Eldred, Jethro, Colville, Adolphus, and Eddy were rabbit trappers who could not afford to attend school in the days when fees were payable; only Eddy could read and write because he had been to Master Tresidder's Night School at the Parish Church School Rooms. Eldred went for one night only but couldn't concentrate, for, as he said, 'I could hear a rabbit screechin' down to Ventongimps.'

Goonhavern cross-roads has long been the traditional focus for much village activity. Here is the inn and here too were the Forge and Fool's Corner, where old and young met to respectively chew the cud and sort out local rivalries with neighbouring villages.

Why the New Inn should be so called is not clear, but the name suggests that it replaced an earlier institution - perhaps because there was already a Kiddlywink in existence. Early photographs date from the time of Percy Westcott who ran the pub and doubled as blacksmith across the road at the old Forge. These pictures show a cottage in front of the public house obscuring the left-hand side of the building. The present pub has integrated the cottage, which now forms the projecting portion of the front of the inn. Early associations are evident because the brewers, J.A. Devenish, used the stables at the rear of the Chapel and two fields opposite.

The Forge, now preserved as a cafeteria, was a busy village blacksmith's shop. In the early 1900s it was run by Joe 'Rudd' Eplett. Besides the farrier's trade, farmers would bring plough shares for sharpening or have new ones made. These were often left outside the shop with their owners' names attached by twine or baling wire.

Outside the Old Forge today is a large flat circular stone called a binding plate. When wooden cartwheels were brought here to have iron tyres affixed, the wheel was centred on the plate and the red-hot metal tyre lowered until it fitted round the rim.
Then came the tricky task of raising the wheel into an upright position and rolling it, like a hoop, to the granite cooling-trough. After a good deal of hissing and steaming, the iron tyre would contract and 'bite' on to the wooden rim.
It was common for 'Rudd' Eplett and later Percy Westcott to deputise as a dentist.

Qualified dental practitioners were few and far between at this time. One local man's grandmother remembered having teeth extracted by 'Rudd', who used a pair of tongs for the purpose. There was no attempt at anaesthetising; one of the men would hold the victim's head firmly, whilst Joe Rudd obtained the necessary leverage on what he hoped was the offending tooth. After extraction, the resulting socket would be sealed with plug tobacco.

The Forge ceased to be a blacksmith's about 1941, and it remained empty and neglected until 1952 when Mr. Jack Nicholls used part of it for a cycle repair shop, and Eldred Greet kept pigs in the other part. In 1955, two sisters took it over and created Tea Rooms, followed in 1959 by the setting up of the present day Old Forge Cafe.

The village was served by Mary Trenerry and her son Jervis who toured the area with a donkey and trap, selling paraffin, soap powders and other household supplies.
The father of the famous Cornish historian and academic, A.L. Rowse, followed the same occupation in the China Clay country near St. Austell. When Rowse stood for election to parliament, he visited St. Dennis to speak. An old man at the back of the hall, determined to take Mr. Rowse down a peg or two, said, 'Do'ee remember when your father used t' come round with 'is donkey and cart selling parafeen and trade?' Rowse replied, 'Indeed I do, sir. Alas for my father, he is dead, but I had no idea the ass came from St. Dennis!'

A much loved character among adults and children alike was Mr. Joseph Reynolds, known to everyone as 'Joey Rhubarb'. With his full white beard, he was for many years sexton, bellringer and organ-blower at the parish church.

Equally well–respected was Mr. Fred Eplett, founder of the Goonhavern Banjo Band and the football and pushball teams, among his many other contributions to village life. After spending many years in Africa, he returned to the village and began the banjo band in 1936. In the course of the next forty years, the Band became famous throughout Cornwall and gave concerts in almost every town and village. One one occasion, the band were booked to play at a remote hall near St. Austell. They lost their way in the dark and finished up outside a large building. Convinced they were at their destination, they flung open the door, only to be confronted by 300 terrified chickens.

The old forge at Goonhavern, about 1918.

The opening of Goonhavern Halt, on the Newquay-Chacewater branch line, opening day, 1903.

SOME WALKS IN THE PARISH

Walkers are well catered for within the parish of Perranzabuloe; there are over 100 footpaths. Laid end to end, they would reach from here to London. The following is a small selection of local walks, from the dramatic clifftops to the quiet valleys, inland.

WALK No. 1.
PERRANPORTH BEACH TO HOLYWELL BAY.

Bathing at Perranporth, 1932.

A stroll along Perranporth Beach is one of the best-loved outings in Mid-Cornwall. Depending on the state of the tide, the walk can be extended to the eastern end of the beach. Keen walkers with a packed lunch will want to go the full 5 miles and take the cliff path through to Holywell Bay.

The starting point is the popular Beach Car Park, built on the site of The Bar where the pilchard fishing boats were once stored. The car park is managed by the Garden Trustees who plough back the revenue into amenities for the public like the boating lake and the conversion of the old railway into a public walkway.

We cross the footbridge over the Perrancombe river and on to the promenade walk. The adjacent area of level grass is now comfortably clear of the sea, but not so many years ago it formed the Inner Beach and the tide swept in, defeating every effort to divide it up with fencing.

Penhale Point and Gull Rock beyond High Cliff.　　　*(Photo: Jack Ingrey.)*

And so to the sands, and a chance to watch the gulls that congregate on the river as it fans out across the beach. Look for the red legs of the Black-headed Gulls, known in Cornwall as River Gulls. Their chocolate-brown heads single them out in the breeding season but at other times they have a distinctive spot behind the eye.

To the right, the sea has carved out low cliffs in front of the Ponsmere Hotel. The present site of the hotel was previously a grassy promontory. Following the discovery of quantities of bones, it is now thought that here was a burial ground for shipwrecked sailors.

A bridge leads over the Ponsmere River. The waters have now been confined to their present channel, whereas they used to occupy a large area of the beach, reaching the sea on the other side of Chapel Rock. Crossing the river before the bridge was built was not so simple, especially when heavy loads of wreck-wood were being hauled by horse and cart. One horseman, Jackie Mitchell, told of a narrow squeak. "Into the sinking sand, down went the load, horse, cart and all, everything was completely out of sight. My dear old Hoss was submerged. I could only see the tips of his ears. I said, 'come up Duke', and he came right out of the river, cart, timber and all."

Heading across the sands, Chapel Rock stands alone on the seaward side, its bulk rapidly diminishing now that the waves have broken over the top. The hermit who lived there centuries ago, tending his warning beacon, would hardly feel at home now.

On the right are the Beach Cafeteria and its amusements, and the Surf Club headquarters with its watchtower. As befits one of Europe's best surf beaches, the Perranporth Club

86

enjoys an international reputation and now travels as far as Australia to compete in surfing and life-saving competitions. The summer service provided by the surf life-guards is invaluable to bathers. Never ignore their advice. The enormous uninterrupted sweep of beach sets dangerous currents in motion. After all, this is not Weston-Super-Mare; this is the mighty Atlantic and it demands respect.

Surfing in 'Perran' goes back to the 1930s when wooden boards were made by the village undertaker, using sheets of white deal and retailing for 2s 6d. The timber merchants in Truro were mystified by the extra orders for floorboarding.

Surf-Riding, to use the old term, can appeal to all ages, and one lady in her eighties daily takes to the surf, even into December. When she alights from her board and walks from the water, there is a spring in her step and she is free from the arthritis that normally plagues her life.

Here in the centre of the beach, scores of shipwrecked vessels have come to grief in the choppy surf. Many keels and anchors lie buried beneath the sands. Ships in trouble way out at sea would aim at this long expanse of sand either in the hope of a soft landing, or, in mistaking it for Padstow Harbour.

Behind the surf club the sand-hills or dunes are being restored and stabilised by plantations of Marram Grass, a deep-rooted plant, said to have been brought to Perranporth by Sir Walter Ralegh.

RAMOTH
The widest part of the beach comes to a finish in a series of sand-filled caves, and some mining excavations connected with Wheal Ramoth tin mine. The rocky outcrops at the seaward end are known fondly as Flat Rocks. The whole village would assemble here on August Bank Holiday for a tea-treat.

Above Flat Rocks, in the grassy slopes, is a platform where a wooden bungalow stood. It was rented by the author, Winston Graham, and he would walk here on winter days to write the Poldark novel, *Demelza* - all the while gaining inspiration from the scenes around. So successfully, in fact, that book sales reached 5 million, television audiences 12 million, and 22 countries broadcast the T.V. series.

If the tide is suitable, the walk can continue along the beach past Flat Rocks; if not, then take the flight of steps up to the hills above. The beach can be regained somewhat further along by means of concrete steps.

Assuming the tide is out, work round the corner of Flat Rocks - Cotty's Point - marking the start of High Cliffs and a series of echoing, dripping caverns which invite a closer look.

The first cave is called Miss Cotty's Vugah, after the Lady of the Manor who enjoyed secluded sunbathing here.

As the cliffs rise in height, Double Caverns are passed leading up to High Cliff Point and Cove. The 'old men' - miners of long ago - have exploited a seam of tin here. Their excavations extend all the way up through the roof of the cave.
Indeed in one of these caves, St. Piran is reputed to have discovered tin, whilst cooking his supper on an open fire. The rock at the floor of the cave heated up and two veins of tin bubbled up white in the form of a cross. Hence St. Piran's Flag, the Cornish National Flag, is a white cross on a black background.

A big colony of Fulmars nests on the cliff ledges, and excellent views of them are available. At first glance they are like gulls, but their thick short neck and straight wings are distinctive. Pairs of Fulmars sit on their chosen ledge and nibble at each other's plumage. Anyone intruding will be showered with an evil-smelling oil which clings like wax; no wonder 'Fulmar' derives from 'Foul-mouth'.

Towards the end of the High Cliffs is a thick, ruddy-coloured vein of quartz extending the full height of the cliff. Its full name is Wheal Byan Cross Course. Next door, water trickles from a mining gallery called Wheal Byan Adit. From here to the concrete steps leading inland the rocks are soft and brittle, and the sea is winning its battle to destroy the land. No doubt when the quartz vein was injected as a red-hot magma, the associated heat, gases and stress so much affected the neighbouring rocks that they now decay and crumble. Events like this explain why the sea has invaded the coastline and scooped out the huge area of Perran Bay.

Just past the concrete steps, the beach is traversed by a windy stream which flows down from Wheal Vlow mine, half a mile yonder in the sand hills. A buttress of hard, green rock called elvan projects forward on the far bank of the stream. As the stream fans out and enters the sea, a flock of seagulls is usually seen feeding, mostly Herring Gulls, but here and there a solitary Great Black-backed Gull.

If you hear a voice from out of the sky, it could conceivably be the ghost of St. Piran, but more probably it will be one of the hang-gliders suspended in the air currents above. Yes, man can fly like a bird - almost.

The furthest reaches of the beach, bounded by the ocean and the dunes, are just about as far from the stress and noise of modern life as it is possible to get in Cornwall today.
The long-distance walker and author, John Hillaby, recalls the exhilaration he felt here. On his journey from Land's End on the way to John O' Groats, he had put behind him the foggy moors around St. Ives, and his spirits soared as he strode across Perran Beach in open

weather. Indeed, the vast endless spaces of sands, sea and sky are enough to make everyday cares of the world seem too small to matter.

It pays to keep one eye on the tideline. Almost anything can be washed ashore, from jellyfish to whales. In 1988, for example, sterling efforts were made to keep alive a Bottlenose Dolphin. In 1932, the schools emptied when a stranded whale was the main event. The warm Gulf Stream from the Carribean sometimes sweeps exotic species thousands of miles off course. In this way, Leatherback Turtles turn up in Newquay fisherman's catches. Likewise, tropical, sun-baked seeds finish up on the beach. Lucky finds include the tan-coloured Sea Purse which can be polished and made into a necklace; the Horse-eye Bean; and the rare seed of the Starnut Palm. This mahogany-black seed is a long-distance floater from the palm-fringed islands of the West Indies.

A spectacular sight is a glimpse of the Peregrine falcons that grace the skies above the dunes and cliffs. The usual view is a distant one becauses the Peregrine sees you well before you see it. Look for a silhouette the shape of an anchor. This precious bird is the world's fastest flier: its vertical stoops can reach 250 m.p.h.

On a quiet day, the typical shoreline birds will be about: perhaps a gang of Turnstones tucked into a sandy recess, Ringed Plovers and gatherings of Sanderlings scampering along the water's edge, or a family group of Oystercatchers on the shingles at the very end of the beach. 'Oystercatcher' is a misnomer. The old name - Musselpecker - would be more accurate. Five hits with the strong, red bill are enough to break open the mussel, and the flesh is cut out using the two halves of the bill like scissors.

As the end of the beach approaches, numerous lumps of rusty iron are found scattered over the foreshore. They are from Gravel Hill Iron Mine, hidden away at the furthest corner of the beach. The coastal path runs around the old excavations. Pillars of iron ore have been left to support the cavernous workings.

The iron exposed in the cliffs shows two branches, separated by a 45 ft. wide 'horse' of older rock. The eastern branch is 15 ft. thick at beach level with a centre of clean ore. Towards the cliff top, it splits into two bands of a foot in width. The southern branch is limonite iron, threaded with quartz veins. We are looking at the northern end of a massive trench of iron, stretching inland for four miles, and known as the Great Perran Iron Lode (see 9). One of the geological highlights of the region, it is slightly younger than the local tin veins - a mere 230 million years old.

Gravel Hill produced 8000 tons of ore in its heyday, 1860-1882. An 11 inch 'puffer' engine drew the iron up the slopes, ready for carting to a purpose-made quay on the Gannel river, three miles away, thence to the smelter in South Wales. Geologists are still making important finds in the quarry. Some rare micro-crystals were reported at the 1988 Rochester Symposium in New York: rare phosphates of iron called ferrostrunzite, beraunite, and eleonirite.

To round off the beach section of the walk, the cliffs leading seawards are worth a closer look. Numerous quartz veins give the clue to the lodes of lead and silver that run right through the headland beyond. Here and there, narrow clefts have been cut by prospecting miners. Low tides allow access to a wonderful area of colourful pebbles and giant boulders. Keen walkers will wish to extend the walk a further three miles to Holywell Bay; they will be rewarded with magnificent views. The route crosses Penhale Army Camp however, and if red flags are hoisted, access will be delayed.

Upon leaving the beach, observe the red noticeboard and proceed for a short distance along the track of the old mine railroad, which boldly heads straight up the hill. Soon an abrupt turn to the left reveals the first of the white marker posts, which indicate the whole of the way ahead.

Waving marram grass gives way to open grassland and there are open views back along the beach and across the bay. Very shortly the first fenced-off mine shaft appears, perched on the cliff edge and signposted with a skull and crossbones! En route to the first headland, Ligger Point, close-range views of the Atlantic rollers are at hand as they wash over a rock islet called The Beagle. At Ligger, as on so many Cornish headlands, there is evidence of early occupation in the form of Bronze Age tumuli or earthmounds.

As the path swings to the right, a marvellous view of Hoblyn's Cove suddenly appears. The high cliffs are shot through with huge veins of bull quartz, and dramatic caverns carved out by man and scoured by the fierce seas. One's respect for the old miners, who won their living in such awesome settings, grows by the minute.

The route proceeds alongside army buildings, but the eye is drawn away to the many zawns or chasms that plummet to the sea below. 'Old men's' shafts sit on the very lip of the cliffs, a sure sign that minerals were abundant. So it proved in the 19th century. Four lodes of lead and silver ran north-south parallel to the coast and they were exploited by the successful mines of Wheal Golden and Penhale (see chapter 9). Their workings ran the length and depth of the whole promontory.

By 1822, Wheal Golden even had its own smelting house, and in that same year, two plates of silver each weighing 60lbs were amongst the ore raised. The sea broke in during 1851; a cement dam was needed to reseal the mine. The company chairman was soon able to report 'not a spoonful of water' remaining, but removing 1000 tons of sand and gravel had used up the year's profits.

Mining buildings almost covered with sand, in dunes near Penhale Point.

In 1870, Penhale Mine employed 200 people, and between 1849 and 1870, 7000 oz. of silver were produced. Output was so good that a ship was purchased to operate from Holywell Bay. Later, ships were actually manoeuvred to the foot of the cliffs and coal hoisted direct to the mine engines. The landing-bay is visible east of Penhale Point. The engine houses were demolished when the army arrived in 1940; a sad loss, because Wheal Golden boasted a castellated stack and was a fine monument at the summit of Penhale. The cliffpath passes beside the Royal Navy Wireless Station where the many bizarre sets of apparatus resemble a play-area for giant children. And so on to the tapering precipes of Penhale Point. Gull Rock now looms up across the narrow sea strait, and we are presented with grand views in every direction: forty miles of coastline from Trevose Head and its lighthouse near to Padstow, down to St. Ives and beyond in the west; inland, Cubert village, and its prominent church spire; and on the southern horizon the China Clay 'Alps'. Holywell beach and bay open out like a minor image of Perran beach.

Penhale Point was a Cliff Castle in the Iron Age and defensive earthworks were strung across the neck of the promontory, adjacent to the boundary of the Wireless Station. There are two parallel 8 feet-high banks and an outer ditch, and at least one iron-age hut dwelling has come to light inside the defended headland. Interesting to reflect that, 2000 years ago on Penhale Point, defence against attack was the main activity here, and that today by courtesy of high technology, it still is!

The descent into Holywell is via the old mine tramway. Halfway down, a concrete base and iron hoops have been installed for Army rock climbing and abseiling practice. It has also become a favourite film location, due in part to the practicability of stationing a generating van at the clifftop. Here the Commercial Union insurance company rolled a car over the cliff and promised in their T.V. advert 'not to make a drama out of a crisis'. The BBC filmed a Dorothy L. Sayers murder mystery here, the body being discovered on a slab of rock on the beach below.

The coastal path swings to the right, and there are pleasant views of the river as it meanders across the marshes at the back of the beach; it is but a short stroll into Holywell village and the end of the outward journey. To return on foot, the route is retraced to Perranporth beach. If the tide has turned and the way past the cliff secion of the beach is barred, then you may bypass this stretch via the concrete steps and the path around the top of the cliffs, thence back down to the beach on the far side, in sight of the Surf Club.

WALK No. 2.
DROSKYN TO CLIGGA HEAD, HANOVER COVE AND ST. AGNES.

Here is a walk described by Poldark author, Winston Graham, as 'Cornwall at its wildest'. The cliffs rise vertically to 300 feet in places and there is a wealth of mining relics. There is no necessity to complete the full five miles; simply take in as much or as little as you please.

A start may be made either from the Beach carpark via Cliff Hill or from Droskyn car park on the green at the top of the hill. From Droskyn, there are grand views of Perran Bay and the the beach. Towards the cliffs is a flat area of public open space lying on a lower shelf of land which is itself a raised beach carved out by the waves of an ancient sea.

Chapel Rock and Cubby Hole.   *(Photo: Steven Cull.)*

The coastline here is dotted with rock stacks and slender arches all formed by the collapse of mine tunnels and galleries which date back centuries. Even before Roman times, erosion of the rocks by the sea would have exposed the minerals and attracted the first miners. In the same way, earlier this century the sands were sorted for tin. A tinner called Billy Rippon made £2 a week using a spade and bucket, and once £40 from a rock fall.

From the roundabout next to Droskyn Castle Hotel, walk up the road beside the hotel and turn right on to the road leading to the Youth Hostel. Looking across to the cliff edge, the land falls away sharply. Before the ground crumbled away, an old mule track hugged the cliff edge and was well used for the carriage of smuggled goods and mine ores.

At Droskyn Point and just before the youth hostel, a flight of steps gives access to an excellent vantage point which has been purpose-built for viewing the coastline. Directly beneath, the waves froth over a slab of rock and shorebirds like Oystercatcher, Turnstones and Purple Sandpipers prospect for shellfish.

Arch formed by mining activity.

The path swings left past an old stone quarry, and out to sea, the Bawden Rocks come into view, nicknamed 'Man and His Man'. Out of sight in the cliffs below are the massive caverns, known by the dramatic Cornish name of Vugah-en-Plunder because of their frequent use by smugglers. They were blessed with their new name of Cathedral Caverns by the first Bishop of Truro. We can appreciate how established smuggling had become, by the fact that a shaft was sunk to connect with the roof of the cavern. Contraband would be hoisted up by a pulley, ready for carting away by donkey.

The path winds its way around the steep inlet of Penwithen Cove and mine shafts are all about. They have been capped with metal grids designed to protect the public and to allow the bats to come and go. The shafts are part of the rich copper mine of Perran Great St. George (see chapter 11).

Once past the cove, the next headland is Penwithen Point where the inrushing waves have been seen to form a blow-hole. Adjoining is Shag Rock which takes its name from the sea birds that perch there. The area of sea enclosed between Penwithen Point and Cligga Head

Wire-capped mine-shafts and adits near Droskyn.

now comes into view. It has earned the name of The Meadow because of its often placid waters - a favourite place to net pilchard shoals in the old days. Even today, fish can assemble in great numbers, and there are occasional gatherings of dive-bombing Gannets.

The path skirts a huge heap of mine waste at the steep sided Wheal East Cove. On the way uphill to Cligga Head, a short turning to the left offers a good view of a mine adit. This damp dark entrance gives a glimpse of what mining conditions were like.

The coastal path now passes through a diverse area, made up of the many derelict buildings which once formed the Explosives Factory, together with the shafts of Cligga Mine, and fortifications from the second world war. This remote site was chosen by a group of Cornish investors who built their British and Colonial Explosives Factory here in 1891. Two years later, the giant Nobel, corporation took over, headed by Alfred Nobel, the founder of the international Peace Prize. The factory sprawled over a wide area of 165 acres so that all the dangerous processes could be isolated from each other.

The hub of the whole plant was the 'Nitroglycerine Hill.' For safety's sake it was sited on the slopes looking out to sea. Among the relics still to be seen is a roofless building drained by a brick-arched tunnel. This was the nitroglycerine nitrator. It was watched over by the nitrator hillman who was given a one-legged stool to sit on, so that if he fell asleep, it would topple over and wake him.

Local people were annoyed when the factory closed off the coastal walk. Matters were made worse by the bombastic manager who acquired the nickname of 'Dynamite Joe'. The factory was felt locally to be bad for the holiday trade, especially in 1902, when a tram was

Remains of the explosives factory, Cligga Head.   (*Photo: Donald R. Rawe.*)

derailed and 500 lbs. of gelignite exploded. Three workmen were killed. Windows rattled in Truro, but a man standing 13 yards away was sheltered by his horse. The poor animal perished but he was not even scratched. The factory was run down in 1905, but during World War I it made munitions and 1000 people were employed.

The tight cluster of mine shafts belongs to Cligga Mine, which differed from others in the district in that it exploited the granite and the swarms of veinlets running through it. Along with tin, the mineral wolfram is present. For a full account of the mine see Chapter 11.

The way forward now is through an old roadstone quarry. Here is a great slab of white rock threaded through with parallel black lines. The rock is granite that has been severely altered by gases and superheated liquids; this altered rock is called Greisen, and this is the best example in Britain. Precious gems such as blue topaz have been found here. A short detour can be made, leaving the quarry to the right of the Greisen exposure, and proceeding around the tip of Cligga Head.

Cligga derives from the Cornish, *Clegar* - a precipice. The land falls away seawards and disappears into a fearful 'zawn' where giant slabs of rock disappear into the sea. Here one must exercise caution and steer clear of the cliff edge, to follow other paths leading to the west side of the headland, from where the first views appear of the sheer 300 feet cliffs and stacks rising out of the inlets called Cliggaporth and Hanover Cove.

Retracing the path back to the quarry, the regular footpath is rejoined and for the next 300 yards spectacular cliff scenery is well displayed. The steep-sided rocks are stained red with

Cliff scene near Cligga Head. *(Photo: Jack Ingrey.)*

iron and yellow with copper, and old miners' tunnels emerge on to death-defying crevices. Those miners also worked the boulder-strewn shores way down below, as recounted by W.J. Henwood in 1838:

'The action of the sea saps the cliff, causing large portions to fall every winter, and several miners earn a living by collecting the particles of tin on the beach. When the tide rises, the miners retire to a hole in a large rock which is surrounded by the sea at high water, and using the salt water, they dress the ores which they have collected, returning to the shore on the reflux of the water.'

On the landward side is Trevellas Airfield, built in 1940 as a base for fighter aircraft whose job was to protect Allied convoys. When 66 Squadron arrived in 1941, the pilots used Man and His Man for target practice.

Approaching the headland of Pen-a-Gader (Chair Head), the shafts and waste heaps of Wheal Prudence begin to appear. It was producing copper in the last century, but in 1862 it failed to live up to its name. The mine captain reported failure due to the decision to drive a shaft into a 'detached and storm-beaten rock.' The shaft was reached along a crumbling, knife-edged path, bordered by a ghastly chasm called 'Old Prison'. Even when a new shaft was sunk 100 yards inland, 'the spray flew over the top of the engine house and the workmen were driven from their posts.'

The fine views from Pen-a-Gader are followed by a walk along the edge of the wartime aerodrome, close by to a pair of aircraft shelters. The first planes stationed here were tipped over by the wind, and protection was needed both from the elements and the threat of enemy attack. The concrete entrance slits have a kink in them to prevent gunfire entering in.

Shortly, the path descends steeply and the delightful valley of Trevellas Coombe is laid out below. The whole scene evokes the mining days of yore. The ruined remains and the absence of any modern development combine to add to the atmosphere. As Winston Graham puts it, 'untouched, unrepaired, undeveloped...' The produce of the giant Blue Hills Mine was sorted through a maze of water-powered contraptions which filled the valley floor. Not surprisingly the coombe was a favourite location for the filming of 'Poldark'. The dark sand of Trevellas Porth still yields enough ore for the manufacture of 'special edition' tin ingots.

Walkers are directed inland by the way marked signs to meet up with a tiny by-road. Its tight hairpin bends were used as a trials section during the London - Lands's End Motor Rally. Crowds of cloth-capped spectators lined the route. Latterly, the road was considered too easy and the cars and motorcycles were directed on to a steep stony track; this is the route that the walk now ascends out of the valley.

At the top, there is more splendid cliff scenery and very soon the sands of Trevaunance Cove, St. Agnes, come into sight. The many engine houses and chimneys of the St. Agnes mining district are set out on the slopes beyond.

A welcome seat is provided to allow views of the cove. The quay here was the outlet for much of the ore mined in Perranporth and surrounding areas, but the sea has now all but obliterated it. At low tide, the broken blocks can be seen piled up like dominoes.

The descending path leads into the cove and journey's end. The main village of St. Agnes is a mile away inland, but there is a hostelry in the cove with an interesting display of seafaring memorabilia, and in the season, a cafe and shop.

WALK NO. 3.
ST. PIRAN'S CHURCH - PENWARTHA COOMBE

A circular country walk, based on the Parish Church, and measuring about 3 miles.

The church is located at Lambourne two miles inland from Perranporth at the junction of the A3075 Newquay Road and the minor road from Perranporth to Bolingey and through Cocks Hill. The name Lambourne appears to be a corruption of the Cornish *Lan*, enclosure, and *bron*, a breast or rise.

St. Piran's third church, built in 1804.   (Photo: Jack Ingrey.)

The whole prospect of church and churchyard is most attractive. Enter through the Lych gate, which contains window tracery and stonework from the old church near St. Piran's oratory. The church itself is often said to have been rebuilt piece by piece from its predecessor in the sand hills, but this is not quite so. When the sands overwhelmed the 12th century Norman church, work on the present church was begun in 1804. Interestingly, the parishioners had been worried about the encroaching sand, a hundred years before in 1704, but the vicar argued that adequate repairs could be made for £2, instead of the £2000 needed for a new church.

The following features of the old church were transferred to the present site: the tower minus the lowest portion, which was left in the sand; the chancel pillars of the arcade; some of the window tracery; the granite font; two slate memorials; and some wood carved panels. The slate memorials on the south wall of the aisle are fine examples of an old Cornish craft. One commemorates a churchwarden, Perran Hoskyn, 1675, and his wife, Elizabeth. The other tablet reveres the Cottey family, Lords of Reen Manor.

View through the lych-gate.   *(Photo: Jack Ingrey.)*

An excellent booklet traces the history of the church and can be purchased by visitors. What is more, the churchyard is full of outstanding 19th century headstones. Opposite the main door is an ancient cross, preserved from St. Piran's oratory–chapel. (See centre pages)

To begin the walk, take the path at the western edge of the churchyard, passing the green gate to the rectory and leaving by an opening at the left-hand corner of the church grounds. We descend into Slads Lane, also called Love Lane, a pleasing thoroughfare enclosed by holly trees and stools of hazel previously coppiced for poles. In spring, a carpet of celandines, violets and primroses adds to the charm. At the end of the lane, progress is made across a series of small fields, all the time hugging the left hand edge of the meadows, and negotiating a number of stone-built Cornish stiles.

At the bottom of the last, steeply sloping field, we enter another lane enclosed by oak and holly. A short descent leads to a crossroads of paths adjacent to a brook and footbridge. An ancient ash tree overlooks this delightful little spot and there is a timeless, unchanged atmosphere. The derelict stone building across the stream was once a Dame School where pupils paid for their instruction before the days of organised education.

Bearing to the right into Lone Lane or School Lane, another splendid walk with oak trees leaning over the brook. The path enters Penwartha Coombe at the side of the former Penwartha School, now a private dwelling. The school (see centre pages), opened in 1879 and closed in 1969, served a wide area of Perranzabuloe parish including Perranporth, which did not have its own school until 1898, and then only a small one. Many local people have affectionate memories of their schooldays deep in the countryside at Penwartha.

The first headmaster, the illustrious Mr. Ashworth, was also a ferocious preacher, so forceful that he once nearly collapsed in the pulpit, sweat pouring from his forehead like drops of blood. He published a book of his poetry under the title, 'Gathered Ears'. Some pupils thought it was a medical book! One poem describes his courting days, and it stands as a tribute to the delights of Penwartha Coombe:

'Neath the hills of Penwartha, the sun has declined,
Though a glory still lingered above,
Like the memory sweet that is left in mind,
When departed our first dream of love.
Calm, indeed, was the hour as we wandered along,
And enriched the soft air with perfume,
While the dear little brook made perpetual song,
For my love and me, there in the Coombe.

(1893)

Bellcote, Penwartha School. *(Photo: Jack Ingrey)*

Many children walked two or three miles to school. Wintertime journeys were adventures begun in darkness. The water chute at the old mill grew long icicles which some children knocked down and sucked as they walked along. Nearby Mrs. Hosking kindly left out a big basket of rosy apples for the passing children and at Nansmellyn Farm, plums were the treat offered.

Rounding the front of the schoolhouse, our own walk along the Coombe is equally pleasant. Shortly before the river bridge, there are two white-washed garages on the right

Nanslone Mill, Penwartha Coombe.   *(Photo: Jack Ingrey)*

hand side. The older of these was another ancient Dame school. A little further on is Nanslone Mill, believed to have been a tuckingmill where homespun cloth was dipped, cleansed and dressed. A waterwheel survives against the wall on the downstream side. The road winds on to the village of Bolingey, but just before Trevellance Cottage, a footpath marker indicates a small path over the stream and into the open fields. The way ahead is up over the hillside with the woods to the right hand side. Higher up, the view opens up to include the lower reaches of the Coombe and the whole of Bolingey and beyond. At the furthermost corner of the field a Cornish stile leads through to a second meadow, and by working round the edge, Slads Lane is eventually rejoined. It is then a short walk back to the church.

The church, north side. *(Photo: Jack Ingrey)*

View from Cocks Hill. *(Photo: Jack Ingrey)*

WALK NO. 4.
PERRANCOMBE - CLIGGA - DROSKYN

A circular walk from the centre of Perranporth, a distance of three to four miles.

The starting point is Lloyds Bank at the start of Boscawen Road. The bank stands on 'Jan Jacka's Corner' where there was formerly a farmyard pond, complete with ducks, geese and perhaps a black horse!

As the village grew, the bank was the first building erected in Boscawen Road. Both the road and the Park alongside bear the name Boscawen - the family name of Viscount Falmouth, whose land this once was. The second building here was the chemist's shop next door. It was originally built for Mr. & Mrs. Polgreen. Their son Ridley Polgreen was a close friend of author Winston Graham, and it was his name that Mr. Graham took and adapted into *Ross Poldark*, the hero of his famous novels.

A hundred yards west, the road forks. Just here is St. Michael's Church, erected as late as the year 1872. The expansion of Perranporth necessitated that the village had a place of worship of its own, bearing in mind that the parish church was two miles distant. Indeed, St. Piran's church remains the mother church, serving the parish of Perranzabuloe as a whole.

The railway bridge opposite is now disused and headless, but the black coping bricks on the wings of the buttresses and the finely crafted stonemasonery of the walls are still to be seen. A pity that such fine building work should have enjoyed an active life of only 60 years. The first train ran in 1903 and the last in 1963 - all within the lifetime of some local people of the time.

The way ahead lies along Perrancombe road, which is the right-hand fork. Alternatively, there is a short diversion available, using the steps provided at the side of the railway bridge. At the top of the embankment, there is a pleasant walk along the old track, fringed by a grove of sycamore trees and here and there buddleias which have escaped from nearby gardens.

Down below to the left is a stretch of the old lane which was cut in two when the railway was constructed - much the same as a modern day motorway carving a path through the countryside. At the end of the lane, the white walls of Nampara cottages show through the trees, isolated from Perrancombe by the building of the railway.

Nampara means 'Valley of Bread'; this was an ancient manor extending along Perrancombe and predating Perranporth as a centre of activity. The name of Nampara will be familiar to viewers of the Poldark series on television, as Ross Poldark's home. Leaving the rail track to the right, via a set of steps, we can rejoin the road along the coombe. The river babbles along beside the road. Meadowsweet and purple loosetrife grow with their roots in the damp soil.

The waters run clear and good views are often available of the many trout and the wriggling eels which swim close to the river banks. Eels will eat almost any animal life and one local lady, who was disposing of fish offal, found she had attracted a pack of twenty hungry eels. The lifecycle of the eel has been a mystery since the days of ancient Greece. We now know, however, that the eels grow to maturity in the rivers and then travel 3000 miles to breed in the Sargasso Sea on the far side of the Atlantic. Only the young, the elvers, make the return journey.

Continue along the road past a side lane that turns off to the right and fords the river. Through this opening, there is a glimpse of the stone-built cottages of Bolenna, another old-established hamlet, its name derived from (Bos), a dwelling, plus a lost Celtic proper name. A little further on, the coombe road runs up a slight incline and then levels out on flat ground. The next turning on the right at White Walls Court leads down a steep slope to a footbridge over the river.

The valley and its attractive stream are nowadays prized for their scenic beauty. Yet not so many years ago the stream was harnessed over much of its course so that it powered all manner of mining apparatus for the crushing and dressing of rock ore, and the coombe gave every appearance of an industrial scene, pervaded by the thump - thump of the long-rodded crushing stamps, rhythmically working up and down and sounding on a still night, 'like the tread of manacled giants'.

After crossing the river, turn left for the path that runs up the side of a massive gulley called The Girt. The onrush of running water scoured out the ground and shaped the steep sides. Possibly an initial channel first formed during the Ice Age when huge volumes of meltwater cascaded from the hills, but, certainly, the gulley owes its present size to the release of water pumped out of the Devonshire Shaft, part of the St. George Mine across the road at the top of the hill. The waters were directed to the combe to provide power for the processing machinery along the valley floor. In those days, the channel was called Susan Tregay's Droke (see chapter 11).

The Droke is choked with young trees with many crab apples, giving a mass of blossom in due season. The luxurious flora in this area section of the walk includes honeysuckle, bluebells, three-cornered leek, pink campions and herb Robert. Cowslips are plentiful in the neighbouring fields. Children on holiday used to make them into cowslip balls. Nowadays however, it is a protected plant and must not be picked. In May, the tall stems

Looking down the Girt, or Susan Tregay's Droke. (Photo: Donald R. Rawle.)

bear drooping clusters of rich yellow bells, and close-up you can see the little reddened spots hiding the nectaries. Shakespeare pays his tribute in *'Midsummer Night's Dream:'*

> The cowslips tall her pensioners be,
> In their gold coats spots you see,
> These be rubies; fairy favours,
> In their freckles live their savours.

Amongst the many charming local names applied to cowslips are St. Peter's Keys, Culver Keys, Palsywort and Galligaskins.

The footpath hugs the left edge of the droke and then crosses over it and widens out into a bigger track. If the walk is to be kept short, the track can be followed to St. George's Hill which runs down into the village. Otherwise, take the stile immediately on the left and walk through a small meadow to the next stile, adjacent to the St. Agnes - Perranporth highway. Before mounting the stile, look for the patch of yellow tufted vetch that flowers in early summer, and observe the lovely sea pinks or thrift which are common on the stone hedges hereabouts in May and early June.

Now cross the main road and take the airfield road directly opposite. Over to the right, lie St. George's Burrows, an area acquired by the parish for public open space and dotted about with tall weathered stacks of mine waste. Here was the site of Perran Great St. George Mine, one of the most profitable in the area. (See chapter 11.)

The road threads between a cluster of neat, stone buildings which survive from the

106

Remains of Perran Great St. George Mine.　　*(Photo: Donald R. Rawle.)*

Explosives Factory, which manufactured dynamite here at the turn of the century. (See Walk no.2)

There is a view along the length of the main airfield runway, which was laid down in a matter of months in 1940 in response to the need for fighters to cover the Western Approaches.

A choice of routes can be negotiated on the way to the cliffs at Cligga Head. This area of low heather and scrubland appears unhospitable, but is nevertheless frequented by many species of birdlife including stonechats, black redstarts and, during spring and autumn migrations, wheatears by the hundred, and exotic passers-by like the wryneck and purple heron.

Approaching the cliffs, a cluster of capped shafts denotes Cligga Mine which was re-opened to produce wolfram, during World War II. Amidst a further scatter of odd structures left behind from the days of the dynamite factory, the coastal path will be encountered on its way from St. Agnes.

Turning right on to the path the route ahead covers the same ground as for the start of Walk no.2, and by means of Wheal East Cove and Penwithen Point and Cove, the path emerges on to the green at Droskyn Point. From here it is a short walk down Cliff Hill to the beach and village centre.

THE LAST WORD

The last word is with Revd. W.Davis Tyack, a 19th century Methodist minister. His quaint description of Perranporth, written in 1886, still rings true:

'Among the watering-places to which the inhabitants of Cornwall resort, for health and recreation, in the sultry summer time, Perranporth, in Perranzabuloe on the north coast, is highly attractive.

'The magnificent sweep of ocean; the fine sweep of beach; the grandeur of the cliffs, natural arches and caverns; the secluded rocks, and retired bathing-places; together with the sandhills, heaths, and grassy slopes, all unite to make it the most fascinating spot. Pleasant is the memory of hours spent exploring the cliffs and caverns; traversing the noble sands; and enjoying rest and converse on those breezy heights and on the rocks by the dashing sea.'

'There is a wildness and yet gentleness and quietude, pervading the scene, which never failed to charm, often as I have paused to admire it.'

REFERENCES

ACTON,R. A View From St. Agnes Beacon.
Landfall Publications, 1989

BIZLEY,M.H. The Church of St. Piran, 1955.

DINES,H.G. The Metalliferous Mining Region of South West England, Vol. I. H.M.S.O., 1956.

FAIRCLOUGH,T. & SHEPHERD, E. Mineral Railways of the West Country. D. Bradford Barton, Truro, 1975.

JENKIN, A.K. Hamilton. The Mines and Miners of Cornwall, Vol.2 St. Agnes to Perranporth, Vol.7 Perranporth to Newquay.
Forge Books, Bracknell.

MARTIN, R.B. Tennyson, The Unquiet Heart.
Faber & Faber, 1980.

PERRANPORTH W.I. The Story of Perranporth School, 1976.

PERRANZABULOE OLD CORNWALL SOCIETY. Place names in the Parish of Perranzabuloe.

RAWE, Donald R. Cornish Villages. Robert Hale Ltd., 1978.

RICKS, C. The Poems of Tennyson, Longman, 1969.

RICKS, C. Tennyson. Macmillan, 1972.

ROBERTS, Capt. William. Perranporth, Cornwall.
Oscar Blackford, Truro, 1939.

SYNGE, P.M. Gardens of Britain - Devon & Cornwall.
Batsford, 1977.

TENNYSON, Hallam. Alfred Lord Tennyson - A Memoir by His Son. Macmillan, 1897.

TOMLIN, E.W.F. In Search of St. Piran. Lodenek Press, Portloe, 1982

TREMEWAN, Tom. Cornish Youth, Memories of a Perran Boy (1895-1910).
Oscar Blackford, Truro, 1968.
A Builder's Life in Perranporth, 1974. Memories of a Perran Man (1918-1938). Blackford, Truro, 1974.

TROUNSON, J. Mining in Cornwall, Vol.2.
Dyllansow Truran, Redruth.

TYACK, W. Davis The Mines of Perranzabuloe.
Hamilton Adams, 1886.